Some thoughts from clients

"In this recession-like economy, ...ative to *low interest rate CD's where principal is guaranteed safe, reduces my annual taxes and is more appealing to me than annuities. I'm much more confident now that I've found it. Thank you!"*

"After meeting with you, we decided on one of your flexible options to make our nest-egg safely work harder for us and CUT our income taxes. We love the guaranteed principal protection with either the potential of up to 12-14% annual interest or getting a 3.95% fixed rate, plus we have easy access to our cash if we ever need it. We're very satisfied."

"No more annual 1099 forms and reaching into my checkbook to pay taxes on CD interest. I've met with a lot of financial planners over the years, yet no one has ever taught me about "opportunity cost". This information was so compelling that I redeemed my largest CD nine months early and gladly took the small interest penalty!"

"I wish these interest income strategies were around 30 years ago. After our second meeting about my prior financial planning, I am re-arranging some of my CD's and I.R.A. investments to take advantage of these tax benefits and get sound potential for higher income. I'm also sharing all of this valuable information with my adult children."

Sound Principles to Follow

- Safety & Security
- Predictability
- Complete Flexibility
- Access & Control

*** TAX EFFICIENCY

Recession-Proof Retirement

A Retirees Guide for Safe Alternatives to CD's, Bonds, Annuities and Mutual Funds to Beat Inflation and Avoid Bear Markets
(Or People Within Five Years of Retiring)

Safely increase interest income now, reduce taxes... or just build more financial security.

Written By:

Mark J. Orr, CFP®

Certified Financial Planner™

and a fee-based Registered Investment Advisor

2050 Marconi Drive Suite #300   Alpharetta, GA 30005
770-777-8309

Another Book (Kindle or paperback) by Mark J. Orr, CFP® is available at Amazon.com:
Search on Amazon.com for - "Stress-Free Retirement Planning"
"Stress-Free Retirement Planning" is written for people that are still saving for retirement (folks in their 20's, 30's, 40's and 50's) that want to totally avoid stock market volatility and risks... and enjoy a substantial future TAX-FREE income stream during their retirement years... and get tax and penalty-free account access along the way.

Join My Financial Planning "Tips" Email list... for more great financial planning and retirement tips.
Simply email your request along with your first and last name to: whitetreemktg@hotmail.com

Please visit and watch relevant videos one of my websites: www.CDandAnnuityKiller.com

3rd Edition -- Copyright 2012

Preface

There have been 23 economic recessions since 1900 and more will follow. They can all adversely and permanently impact a retiree's lifestyle and/or their hopes for leaving a meaningful legacy. On average, one happens about every five years, so you will likely experience 5-7 recessions during your retirement. Have you recovered from the last two yet? Are you fully prepared for the next one?

With that in mind, retirees need secure places to put their money that provide decent returns that safely beat inflation, great liquidity and more. In this book, you will learn all about a great CD, bond, annuity and mutual fund alternative. I hope that you will enjoy this educational information!

A Request for Your Book Review on Amazon!

Thank you for downloading this e-book. Please REVIEW this book on the Amazon.com website so that I can make the next version even more valuable.

Thank you very much for your help and participation!

Table of Contents

"Safe Money" Strategies to Fully Prepare For the Next Recession, Reduce Your Taxes… Or To Raise Your Interest Income Now

As a financial planner, I meet with retirees every week who complain or worry about the very low recession-induced CD and bond interest rates. But seldom do I meet someone who has any idea of what their "safe" Certificates of Deposit are really "costing" them by reducing their current lifestyle and their net worth (less prepared for the next recession).

Whether you depend on interest income from your CDs, bonds, annuities or mutual funds or you simply let your interest rollover into the next CD, this book provides flexible recession-proofing solutions for either "boom or bust" economies. One solution does <u>not</u> involve taking stock market or bond risks but the I.R.S. will not allow I.R.A.'s to participate.

The other solution (perfect for I.R.A.'s or annuities with large embedded gains) has an impressive historical track record of relatively low risks (with only small and brief fluctuations in account values) in order to get steady returns of 6½% - 7½% over the next 5, 10 or 15 years.

In both cases, we guard against the effects of recessions and take full advantage of the booms in order to combat inflation – which is a retiree's biggest risk if they live a long life. Put another way, my overall financial planning process always revolves around being fully defensive and prepared for the bad times - yet always ready and opportunistic for the good times.

The next paragraph is such a key point for this book (and for your own retirement success), that I will repeat it once again. It's so important to understand how recessions and the resultant bear markets can destroy your retirement dreams and legacy goals.

There have been **23 economic recessions since 1900 and more will follow**. Some are much more severe than others, yet they can all be harmful and adversely impact retiree's lifestyle and/or hopes for leaving a meaningful legacy. On average, **one happens about every five years, so you will likely experience about 5-7 of them during your retirement**. Each recession we endure can permanently damage our retirement lifestyle and/or legacy.

When they do occur, income from interest earnings will drop along with the stock market. Since we know they will keep coming, let's get fully prepared, properly protected and ready to make a profit. But you have two other retirement risks to prepare and plan for as well.

Longevity and Inflation Risks

Let's be clear: along with the high likelihood of living through a number of future recessions, longevity and inflation are the big demons to beat during retirement.

Many retirees have yet to fully consider, plan and invest for these nearly inevitable occurrences. That could be an awful mistake unless you have a million dollars in savings, a large pension that you *both can count on*… and you don't rely on two Social Security checks each month. What will happen when one of those Social Security checks stops coming in?

The average lifespan of retired Americans has been rising for many decades and will continue to do so as medical advances keep us alive longer. A couple aged 62 today, has a joint life expectancy of age 92. That means at least one of them is likely to live until age 92 or even longer. So we should really plan for a 25-35 year retirement income stream.

However, we can't forget about inflation risk over the next few decades. Every year, everything that you will need to buy will cost more. At just 3% inflation, your cost of living will double in 24 years. At 4% inflation, your living costs will double in just 18 years. **With inflation factored in, we need to plan for a 25-35 year "*rising income*" -- as your cost of living will probably double**. For many people, that's a big future financial issue to face. One cannot afford to wait and deal with this looming economic "time-bomb" later.

There are currently 97,000 Americans that are at least 100 years old and that figure will double every decade going forward. You or your spouse could easily be one of them if you enjoy great health today. So *planning for a rising retirement income stream* that lasts until age 100 is the only prudent thing to do, as nobody wants to outlive their savings.

In thinking about your own retirement, does it seem "more probable" to you that your money will outlive you… or that you will outlive your money? What's your gut feeling?

In either case, by investing some time to read this book, I'm confident that you will learn some very sound retirement strategies and timely ideas that can substantially improve wherever you financially "are" at this point in your life. You probably have few financial worries or concerns right now and you have earned that financial peace of mind. You don't need to take big risks with your capital at this stage and you probably shouldn't.

But… your money can safely work much harder for you. Each dollar and investment should have a defined "job description". In these uncertain and so-called *new-normal* economic times, it's a great idea to learn different wealth, investment and tax strategies.

My name is Mark Orr and, I've been a practicing Certified Financial Planner™ and an experienced *fee-based* Registered Investment Advisor since 1998. I've helped cautious seniors across the country recession-proof and increase their retirement income, enlarge their legacy and safely lowered their income taxes – while usually slashing their investment risks.

In addition to sharing my personal financial beliefs, values, ideas and insights with you, I'll also introduce you to an *alternative use* of a powerful financial tool that can make your wealth do "double and triple duties" for you and substantially decrease your annual income taxes or can **increase your interest income** to help you beat inflation and recessions.

Whether you intend to use your interest income for living expenses or just continue to save it all and hope that you'll never need it, I'll give you a number of interesting client examples to show you how and why this proven retirement plan strategy can be a much better and more flexible alternative to CD's, bonds, annuities or even risky mutual funds.

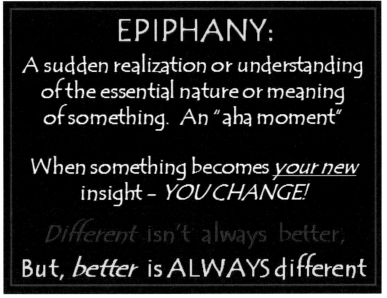

EPIPHANY:
A sudden realization or understanding of the essential nature or meaning of something. An "aha moment"

When something becomes *your new* insight – *YOU CHANGE!*

Different isn't always better,

But, *better* is ALWAYS different

The Federal Reserve says that "interest rates will remain low through at least 2014".

"Financial planning" is a simple and focused process to meet a stated financial need. It's not a product sale. Financial products are only "tools" that professional planners use to satisfy or meet a client's specific goal, objective or aspiration. With that said, here we go...

In all economic times, both good and bad, retirees use certificates of deposit, bonds, money market funds, savings accounts and fixed annuities as very safe and liquid places to protect their money. They also turn to these types of investments to earn "reliable" interest income to support their retirement lifestyle. They haven't been so reliable lately.

In bad times or recessions, when the stock market and home prices are crashing, more investor money ends up in these types of safe financial vehicles than ever, as investors run for cover. When that happens, interest rates drop dramatically (for most people) so you earn far less than you did before. For many, the financial repercussions are substantial.

When those types of investments are paying just 1%-5% interest rates, despite the safety of principal, retirees aren't very happy with those low returns. And when you add paying income taxes on your CD interest, both the after-tax interest returns along with the loss of your REAL purchasing power that inflation causes, the overall net return... is downright pitiful. You may not "feel" inflation much today - but you sure will over time.

If you need $60,000 to live on and enjoy retirement today, at just 3% inflation, your cost of living will rise to $120,000 per year in 24 years. At 4% inflation, your living costs will reach that figure in just 18 years.

Using the figures above, if you are 65 today and living on $60,000, then your annual income will need to climb and double to $120,000 at age 89. How will your CD's and bonds keep up? They can't.

You have every reason to be very careful and prudent with your money. Yet the ever-rising costs of living are a very real threat to your financial comfort and security over the long term. And with constant advances in medicine, you'll likely be retired for many years.   If your income is mostly "fixed", inflation will slowly destroy your purchasing power. Most folks *cannot avoid taking any risks* (CDs) as their income eventually suffers from low rates.

Now let's examine a very expensive problem that you likely don't even realize that you have. Over time, it can adversely impact your overall wealth, financial independence, economic well-being and your readiness for the next recession. The costly dilemma is… how much money is your non-IRA CD's, bonds and any other taxable investments actually "costing" you and your heirs -- ***if you are not spending the interest income they earn now***?

How much money are your CD's, bonds and taxable mutual funds actually… costing you?

Let's say you have $100,000 sitting in taxable CD's, bonds or funds and like many of my clients, you never touch the principal or the interest they earn. In fact, you don't even pay the income taxes due on the interest out of this account. You just re-invest the interest back into the principal and roll it all back into the next CD.

Long-term inflation is actually eroding its "real value" as is the damaging effect of paying annual income taxes out-of-your-pocket. So why not put your money to work for your own and your loved one's benefit… rather than for the bank's?

I understand that CD and most bond interest rates aren't 4%-5% now and haven't been that high for a while, but would you agree that over most normal economic times, that's a pretty average figure? The concepts below will apply to taxable mutual funds too.

Quite frankly it doesn't matter what interest rates are, as the problem is the same whether CD rates are 2% or 10% - they *usually reflect "official CPI" inflation*. In the best case scenario, even before paying income taxes, you are simply treading water in purchasing power. In times like the present, many say they are going "broke" slowly. Do you believe the "official" CPI numbers? My cost of living is rising faster than that.

A note on taxes: Taxable income above $35,350 if you are single or $70,700 if you're married puts you in the 25% tax bracket. At the 31% marginal tax bracket (25% federal plus 6% state) you'll owe $1,550 in taxes on that extra $5,000 of taxable interest income.

So in the first year your CD or bond earns $5,000 and you roll back the interest into the CD which now has a principal of $105,000 earning 5% for the next year. Then you are going to get a 1099 form from your bank saying that you owe taxes on this year's $5,000 income.

Like most of my retired clients, you probably pay those income taxes right out of your checkbook -- instead of touching the principal of your CDs, bonds or taxable mutual funds. Most people don't realize the full magnitude of the total amount of tax dollars that over time, they have "transferred" away from their everyday personal lifestyle and/or wealth... over to the government. It really adds up over the years and is quite disturbing to many.

Five years have gone by and your CD is now worth $127,586. The 1099 form for this year says that you owe taxes of $1, 884. Over just five years you've written checks for a total of $8,565 out of your personal funds to pay for income taxes on CD, bond or fund interest. I call these personal funds your "lifestyle" money. How do you feel about this?

Let's fast forward again. In just 12 years your CD or fund is now worth $179,586. Your tax bill for that year's interest is now $2,651. Over the past dozen years you have paid $24,672 in taxes out of your "lifestyle" money – just to grow your CD savings to $179,586. The picture grows worse every year going forward as the checks to pay the annual tax bills get bigger quickly. The "true cost" of owning CD's becomes larger and larger each year.

As your taxable savings grows, so does the *annual income tax liability* to get you there (whether we're in a recession or not). At some point, most people won't pay able to keep paying the increasingly larger tax bills out of their fixed monthly income and they will have to "raid" their CD principal, savings, bond or fund portfolio to pay the piper (the I.R.S).

Again, I understand that interest rates aren't 5% right now (except for my own clients) – so the tax amounts wouldn't be as bad today. But keep in mind... I'm also only using $100,000 in this example. You likely have much more money in CD's, bonds, T-bills, savings accounts and mutual funds than that. Saving tax dollars can allow our nest-egg to recover.

What did that $24,672 of unnecessary income taxes cost you in your lifestyle? How many extra cruises, family reunion vacations or new life experiences would that amount of taxes buy for you? How many wonderful gifts to your grandchildren or larger donations to your favorite charities? How much better prepared could you be for the next recession?

That's a very significant and totally unnecessary personal wealth transfer to the I.R.S. which we can easily put an end to. Have you ever stopped and thought about how many tens of thousands of dollars from your checkbook that you have needlessly sent to the I.R.S. on interest earnings that you were not spending? Has your CPA ever calculated this exact figure for you? Has that income caused your Social Security checks to be taxed?

Lost "Opportunity Costs" can be expensive

This "financial mistake" gets even worse than this for anyone who just rolls any taxable interest back into the CD, savings account or mutual funds and pays the income taxes out of their checkbook, as I'll explain next. Opportunity cost is an "unseen but very real" economic concept that applies to each and every single financial decision that you make.

Here's what "opportunity cost" means to you in this circumstance. If you pay one dollar in taxes that you did NOT have to pay, you not only LOSE that dollar, but you lose the interest that "tax dollar" could have EARNED for you for many years to come. Going back to our earlier example, if you didn't have to pay nearly $25,000 in taxes over those 12 years on the CD interest, those dollars could have earned interest as well.

At the same 5% interest rate over those twelve years, your "opportunity cost" on paying those very unnecessary tax dollars was $7,141 --- lost to you and your heirs forever. So your CD value is now worth nearly $180,000. However, the true cost for you to have and enjoy that gain in value was a combined $31,812 in taxes and lost opportunity cost. That's a great deal of money and means it actually "cost" your lifestyle, wealth or future legacy nearly $32,000 to have your CD grow to $180,000 over a dozen years.

You can likely "afford" this significant loss and cost, but should you continue to pay it? Once my senior clients fully understand the above, they nearly always ask me for prudent alternatives which would consistently and safely provide them with 4%-6% or even higher interest rates while avoiding the very real and painful $31,812 of costs to get them there.

Countless retirees look to tax-deferred annuities to solve this financial dilemma. But for many retirees, with today's low rates – most fixed annuities are not appealing at all.

So what is a risk-adverse investor to do with money that's most likely earmarked to be passed along to your family and in the meantime, is only earning "peanuts" at the bank or in bonds? How can you stop paying $1,000's of unnecessary income taxes out of your checkbook every year and losing valuable opportunity costs that reduce your present lifestyle, charitable giving and your legacy… or simply decrease your available resources?

Where can you store your savings to preserve and safely recover and grow your capital without fearing the loss of your principal if you ever needed those funds for any reason?

A few more words about bonds

In the proceeding paragraphs, I focused the comments on CD's which generally pay lower interest rates than most bonds do. Bonds usually pay higher rates of interest since they are subject to various potential principal risks. One risk to principal is that it's possible and not even rare that a bond could default. Default doesn't happen with US government bonds, but municipal bonds and corporate bonds do share that investment risk.

Another principal risk that bonds can easily suffer from is "price risk". The prices or values of most every bond can go up and down until they mature due to a number of factors. Those factors can include changes in interest rates, the financial strength of the bond issuer, etc. For example, when interest rates rise, all things being equal, the price of the bonds will generally fall. The opposite effect takes place when interest rates drop. Or when a city, or county runs into fiscal difficulty, their debt may be downgraded and hence the value (prices) of their issued bonds would likely fall. That would not be good if you ever needed to sell them

Let me ask you, are interest rates more likely to go up right now... or go lower? There sure isn't too much room for them to fall is there? Most economists just say it's a matter of time and by how much interest rates will go up, not "if" they will rise.

So if rates are more likely to go up (maybe in 2-4 years), what is going to happen to the price or value of those bonds, if you want to or need to sell them before they mature? They are probably going to drop in value. Most retirees don't want to see their bond holdings drop in value – no matter how secure the interest income stream might be.

Another risk to the value of a bond is default risk. Who would have seen the Enron, WorldCom or many cities in America default on their bonds coming? You usually don't know until it's too late. And when YOU do know, I can guarantee that the bond professionals and Wall Street have already dumped those bonds and there will be few buyers to take them off your hands before maturity – assuming the issuing entity has the funds to pay you back at that point.

One final bond risk (and applies to CD's too) that I'll mention here is inflation risk – especially if you are spending your bond interest income each year. When you buy a bond for $1,000 that will mature in 15 years, what is that $1,000 bond going to be worth in purchasing power at that time? Well if inflation is 3%, then the present value of that bond in the future or what it will buy in today's money at maturity is only $642. Did you stockbroker ever explain that to you?

I'm not suggesting that bonds are bad and that you shouldn't own them. I just want you to fully understand them better so you will see the risks and potential pitfalls.

Wealth and Lifestyle Preservation

First and foremost, we want to preserve your financial well-being, safely grow and compound your assets to fight the adverse effects of the rising costs of living... and then maximize the future gift to your loved ones should you never need those particular funds.

We also want to avoid the $10,000's (taxes) in actual lost wealth that your CD's are costing you if you aren't spending your interest every year... or safely increase your present interest income if you are. These timeless concepts will help you maintain your financial independence and are the guiding compass for all of the strategies described in this report.

What if you could keep some of your money in a secure place, where there was no risk to principal due to losses in the stock market, declines in real estate values or being fully exposed to lower bond prices when interest rates rise?

And what if those funds could earn a guaranteed MINIMUM of zero to 1% interest in the absolute worst years... and yet safely earn up to 12%-14% in the good years? That wealth planning idea sounds pretty good, doesn't it? This account growth can help you recover from the last two recessions.

Your account balance can never go backwards or negative due to stock market returns, yet it has the annual upside potential of earning a robust double-digit return. Even better than that, your yearly interest gains are then locked-in and become principal and are then shielded from any future losses.

Whether those annual interest gains are 1%, 6%, 11% or 14%, they can never be lost or "given back" to the market. They become part of your protected principal that you can absolutely count on in the future.

In a few moments I'll explain about one of the two methods (the "index" strategy) of how interest is credited to your account -- that can transform your retirement. The other method is a "fixed interest rate" (currently 3.95%) which is similar to a money market fund.

And just like an annuity, what if you didn't have to pay annual income taxes on those earnings until you spend it? That is called deferred taxes. And your interest earns interest – all tax deferred. Unlike CD's and bonds, you do _not_ get a 1099 in the mail with a big tax bill to pay by April 15th. **You can even reduce your quarterly I.R.S. estimate checks now**!

Since there is no income tax bill to pay (either out of your lifestyle money or from the account itself)... there is no "opportunity cost" incurred. You keep more wealth.

Nor does the growth of your account cause your Social Security income to be taxed. Not even municipal bonds can do that for you. It sounds like an annuity? But this is not an annuity. For many seniors in this situation, it's so much better for you and your loved ones.

Whether you choose the fixed interest rate or the "index" strategy, your funds are held by some of the largest and highest-rated "mutual" insurance companies that have served their policyholders for well over 100 years. Your money is very safe and secure.

That's why $700 million dollars went into this "recession-proof" retirement strategy in 2010 and nearly **$930 million was invested in 2011**. Ten large U.S. banks have over $60 BILLION invested in this "asset class" for their Federal Reserve "Tier 1 Capital requirements" too. Why not look for better opportunities to navigate these uncertain economic times like so many others have?

Rising income taxes

Let me quickly write about income taxes. You were probably told that your tax rate would always be lower in retirement. Given our disturbing and growing national, state and local deficits, do you think that your taxes will be going up in the next few years?

With the US National debt at some $16 TRILLION dollars and spiraling out of control, most people believe that taxes will have to go higher at some point. When you add the more than $51 TRILLION dollars in un-funded Social Security, Medicare and Medicaid promises made, each and every American citizen's share of the national debt and these future liabilities is about $200,000 and counting.

The National Debt is now $16 Trillion

12/15/2011

Medicare	- $24.8
Soc. Sec.	- $21.4
Fed Debt	- $9.4
Military Retire.	- $3.6
Fed. Emp. Retire.	- $2.0
State & Local	- $5.2

Total $ 66.4
Trillion dollars OWED!

$16 TRILLION dollars of USA debt owed PLUS ADD over $51 Trillion of the un-funded -- yet promised liabilities of Social Security, Medicare and Medicaid!!

Our national debt is rising by more than $3 million every single minute ($4 BILLION a day)

Take a look at the chart on the next page for the history of the top marginal tax rates. Since 1913 the "average" top marginal tax brackets averaged over 50%. Would you bet on lower taxes in the future – especially if you have high taxable income? Here's an example of a *new tax law that's already passed*.

Unless Congress makes a change, **effective in 2013, a new law will subject those with high incomes (over $200,000) with a 3.8% additional Medicare contribution (tax)** on ALL unearned income (interest, rents, dividends, etc.).

Currently, the top federal bracket is "only" 35%. You'll notice that taxes tend to go up when we need to pay for wars like WWI, WWII and the Korean War. What's missing? The two wars we are waging today in Afghanistan and against terrorism (plus we're still paying for the war in Iraq). They've already cost our country two trillion dollars.   Below, let's see what $1 million, $1 billion and $15 trillion look like in actual piles of cash.

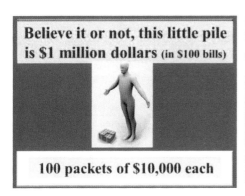

Believe it or not, this little pile is $1 million dollars (in $100 bills)

100 packets of $10,000 each

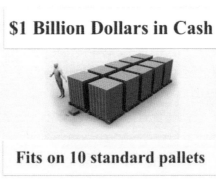

$1 Billion Dollars in Cash

Fits on 10 standard pallets

$15 Trillion Dollars in Cash!

Topped $15 Trillion in U.S. Debt 2 months before Christmas 2011

This depiction of $15 TRILLION dollars (piles of cash) is scary and our nation owes more than that already and growing so fast. Isn't it likely that tax rates are going to go up?

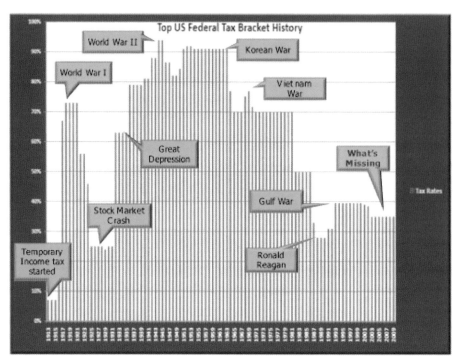

Top Marginal Income Tax Rates From 1913 Range from 8% - 94%

No matter what your political beliefs are, the money has to come from somewhere eventually, and the likely bet for many is that the "so-called rich" (you and me), will pay higher income taxes – maybe a lot more. There are even new proposals in Congress to tax *dividends on stocks at your <u>highest</u> tax bracket rate*. What's next? Many folks want to take practical steps now to prevent potentially higher income tax bills down the road.

If tax rates do go up, those annual checks that you write out of your lifestyle money (from your checkbook) on the CD/bond interest earnings that you are not spending are going to get even more painful. And so are the corresponding lost opportunity costs.

Are you currently spending your interest earnings? Then I am sure that you would like to maximize your net "after-tax" spendable income from your savings – even if your tax rates do go higher soon? Why not give yourself an after-tax "raise" today?

It's our patriotic duty to pay our "fair share" as good Americans. It's the right thing to do. However, the I.R.S. tax code (71,684 pages in length) says that we only have to pay what we legally owe under the current tax laws and not one penny more. We have the absolute right to legally reduce our annual tax bill to the lowest amount allowed, by strictly obeying the I.R.S. regulations. Just like portfolio diversification, we need tax diversification.

Each unnecessary tax dollar sent to the government is gone forever. Conversely, a "tax dollar" saved is a dollar earned. The dollars kept in your own pocket can earn interest. Doing more "good" for your fellow man is called... charity. You direct your money to the exact charity or cause that you want it to go to. You control where your money goes and how it's spent. You will actually enjoy seeing the "good" work that your donated dollars are doing for others. Plus you even get a nice big tax deduction too. That's so much better.

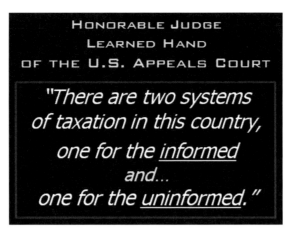

**We have the absolute right to legally reduce our tax bill
to the lowest amount allowed by law**

Which person do you think pays lower income taxes, the informed person... or the uninformed person? The proactive individual... or the submissive one?

You know that smart people legally pay lower taxes because they understand the tax system or hire a financial advisor that does. With my help, even your "non-qualified" (non-I.R.A.) brokerage accounts can get significant tax-relief, as well as earn higher returns with much less risk.

Unless your CD's, T-bills, bonds and money market accounts are in an I.R.A., you are paying taxes on the interest every single year. I've already mentioned that like an annuity, this wealth preservation tool offers tax-deferral to save you $10,000's in taxes over time.

However, this tax and wealth strategy can get even better in some cases. Instead of being just tax-deferred, we can potentially make all of your interest 100% tax-free when you access it by making some simple adjustments. Tax-free income is much better than tax-deferred – but this *only applies* if you don't plan on spending your CD or bond interest until sometime in the future. I'll explain more about that possibility later.

Ok, so exactly what is <u>one</u> of the safe financial products that I work with that handily beats CD's, bonds, annuities and mutual funds? What kind of very conservative financial vehicle can securely provide you with all of these formidable benefits to safely maximize and retain every dollar that you worked so hard for and accumulated over the years?

Believe it or not, this recession-proof and monthly income "recovery tool" is a properly constructed **"SINGLE PREMIUM" LIFE INSURANCE POLICY**. And more specifically here, it's a single premium indexed universal life insurance contract – also known as an IUL.

We could also use a specially-designed single-premium <u>whole life</u> insurance policy instead, although an IUL can perform much better for you and your family. However, both of these dependable, conservative financial products can make an immediate and significant improvement on your monthly income, taxes, your wealth and your legacy.

Ed Slott is a CPA and THE nationally recognized expert on I.R.A.'s. Not only did he write a best-selling book "The Retirement Savings Time Bomb and How to Diffuse It", his educational television specials can regularly can be watched on Public Broadcasting Stations (PBS) across the country. He knows his stuff.

In his book he writes, "I'm not a shill for the life insurance industry – I don't sell life insurance… It is important to look at life insurance… as a solution to a problem."

As you read further, you'll discover a little known fact that the first and primary beneficiary of your own life insurance policy should be yourself. That's right, it's YOU that can benefit most from owning an IUL – not necessarily your beneficiaries.

An Indexed Universal Life Policy – also called an IUL

Now don't let the words "life insurance" put you off one tiny bit – or you will really miss out. **You'll soon discover that all IUL's safely earned more than +8.98% of interest in 2003, 2004, 2006, 2009 and 2010 – with no stock market or bond risk to your principal**.

That's right, in 75%-85% of the time this type of specially designed <u>single-premium</u> life insurance policy will reduce your annual income taxes, compound your wealth to vigorously fight inflation and better meet most all of your financial goals by a very wide margin compared to "lazy" CD's, bonds and even diversified but still risky mutual funds.

Here's a quick example of using a single-premium IUL as a CD alternative. Then I'll write more about how they work and all of the benefits that a properly structured IUL (or a whole life policy) can give to you and your family. Remember that you can <u>stop</u> writing $10,000's in checks to pay for income taxes as well as avoid "lost" opportunity costs.

Let's imagine that you are a 75 year old male in good health with money sitting in CD's that is earning "peanuts" – even before considering income taxes and inflation.

If you simply "re-positioned" some of your money, perhaps $100,000, from a taxable CD and made a "one-time" $100,000 premium payment into a great IUL contract from a very highly-rated mutual life insurance company, your immediate death benefit would be about $160,000. We instantly created $60,000 more money to add to your legacy.

Yet there are so many more benefits to this smart financial move than just getting the larger death benefit for your spouse or family, as you'll soon see. **There is a multitude of very powerful "living" financial and tax planning benefits plus tremendous financial flexibility including tax deferral and 7%-8% average returns with no stock-market risk**.

Keep in mind that *in this example*, this CD money was earmarked to be passed on to your children if you never used it and it is not needed to provide for your current lifestyle. So you have immediately increased your legacy by 60% and there's no future income taxes paid by you or the beneficiary.

How many years of earning 2%-5% and then paying taxes annually, would it take for a $100,000 taxable CD to grow to $160,000 tax free?

Don't forget that your single premium payment put into your policy earns interest too. Over the last 25 years, even including recessions and through 5 bear markets, the historical average annual return of this IUL policy would have been over 7.9% tax-deferred.

Even during 2000-2009, which was actually the worst decade for the stock market since the Depression, this IUL's "index" strategy would have safely credited nearly 7% a year on average – without any painful capital losses ever.

Using a conservative 7.5% average annual return, not only would the cash value in your IUL policy grow, and so would the tax-free death benefit. In just 12 years the income tax-free death benefit could grow to roughly $200,000. That's twice as much as your single premium payment of $100,000.   And just like an annuity, you do not get any annual 1099 forms in the mail, so you save thousands of dollars of income taxes over time. You keep more money in your checkbook or simply improve your retirement lifestyle now.

At the same average return, your tax-free legacy could grow to about $300,000 by your mid 90's – tripling your single premium. Meanwhile, the interest in a CD would still be fully taxable every year (you will have paid $10,000's of taxes along the way). The CD is not likely to ever keep up -- even if the ½%-2% rates that Fed Chairman Ben Bernanke has told us will remain for at least two more years begin to rise to more "normal" levels.

I'm sure that you are impressed with how this policy can safely multiply your legacy in any economic environment (as well as totally avoid the costs and delays of probate).

But what happens if you ever need access to and the use of the CASH SURRENDER VALUE in your policy for any reason? **Not only does the death benefit grow… so does your cash account value (your new and much more flexible emergency fund).**

You could take out a big lump sum or just take a little out at a time. It's a very safe and liquid place to keep your excess cash. You enjoy attractive, tax-deferred rates of return with no principal risk.

This safe and effective "CD substitute" provides multiple financial benefits – all at once. Should future inflation become rampant and at age 90 you needed to take some income out of your policy to keep up with your higher living expenses, you can do that.

Under those same expectations, you could take out $2,000 every month from your policy until age 105 and still leave a small death benefit for your heirs. If you took $2,000 income a month out of your policy for ten years, that would total $240,000 income over that time period. CD's wouldn't have a chance at equaling that performance.

It's a great emergency fund if you ever need it -- and the greatest tax-free wealth transfer vehicle if you don't. When you really think about it, it certainly makes sense to take an early withdrawal penalty on CD's to add much more flexibility to your financial life.

Just about every senior can save taxes and enjoy higher safe annual returns this way. A whole life insurance policy or an IUL can usually be issued and be a very attractive multi-purpose alternative to CD's and bonds up until the age of 90. The previous example was for a 75 year old male in very good health. If he was in excellent health or was younger than age 75, the numbers just discussed would be even better.

And since women usually live longer than men, the results can be more impressive when a woman is the insured. Even better financial outcomes can occur when both the husband and wife are insured under one "survivorship" policy.

If you have some very serious health issues (are uninsurable), you can still enjoy the tax-deferral and all of the other benefits of life insurance. We simply insure your spouse, a sibling or an adult child. Yet YOU can keep full ownership of and complete control over all of the decisions regarding the policy, including using any of the cash value, taking monthly interest income and making all beneficiary designations.

A properly structured IUL can safely grow your cash reserves much faster than a CD or a tax-deferred annuity with principal protection. If providing yourself with a tax-free income stream down the road is something that interests you more than the size of your future legacy, we can easily design your IUL to do that for you under I.R.S. code 72(e).

An example of an IUL working for Joseph

Joseph was a healthy 65 year old male client with $250,000 sitting in low-interest and taxable CD's. He didn't need to touch the principal or interest yet he wanted easy liquidity. In fact, he was really tired of writing checks out of his checkbook to pay for the income taxes to the I.R.S. and the State of Georgia on the interest that these CD's generated.

He was also quite unhappy with the dreadfully low interest rate his bank was paying him for the last few years – while lending out his money at 12%-29% to credit card holders and constantly nickel and diming his bank accounts.

After I showed him how much money his "opportunity cost" was on those tax dollars, I could see the light bulb turn-on in his head. He got it. He understood there's a much better financial road to meet his financial aspirations than one-dimensional and taxable CD's. He quickly decided to move his $250,000 into an IUL contract with an initial income tax-free death benefit of $545,000.

He wanted his cash to be very safe and to be liquid just in case he needed it – and not produce any more taxable income. His wife also liked the financial protection of the death benefit which more than doubled his cash instantly.

Comparison Between the S&P Index and the Index Universal Life (IUL) Contract for 12 years

Year	Historical S&P 500 Return	$100,000 Basis	Index Universal Life Policy	$100,000 Basis
1999	19.50%	$119,500	13.00%	$113,000
2000	-10.14%	$107,383	1.00%	$114,130
2001	-13.04%	$93,380	1.00%	$115,271
2002	-23.37%	$71,557	1.00%	$116,424
2003	26.38%	$90,434	13.00%	$131,559
2004	8.99%	$98,564	8.99%	$143,386
2005	3.00%	$101,521	3.00%	$147,687
2006	13.62%	$115,348	13.00%	$166,886
2007	3.53%	$119,420	3.53%	$172,777
2008	-38.50%	$73,443	1.00%	$174,505
2009	23.50%	$90,703	13.00%	$197,190
2010	12.80%	$102,312	12.80%	$222,431
Acct Balance		$102,312		$222,431
Avg ROR	0.19%		6.9%	

The IUL Had NO Negative Years – EVEN During the Recessions!
All Past Annual Gains Were Locked-in and Protected From Future Losses
Compare The S&P 500 Index's 0.19% Average Annual Return With 7.24% in the IUL
(Using a 13% Cap and a 1% Floor)

Even illustrating an annual average interest crediting of 7% (which this policy would have _actually_ credited during 1999-2011) the cash surrender value in his contract would have grown from $250,000... to about $471,000 in just 13 years. Plus it's all tax-deferred.

And that impressive growth is AFTER DEDUCTING ALL of the insurance policy loads, fees and charges. His CD money is now safely delivering more value for him and his family. His annual tax bill decreased, he's earning a higher return and there's a death benefit too.

I'll explain exactly how the simple yet impressive "index interest strategy" works in a moment. The main thing to understand is how well this IUL policy performed during a time that included the worst full decade of the stock market since the Depression and through two recessions (2000-2009) -- without taking any stock or bond market risk. Your principal never experiences a negative annual return due to market crashes or recessions. Never.

The previous chart shows a comparison of the raw S&P 500 index (middle column) to an IUL (far right column) with both options starting with $100,000 on 01/01/1999 and going through 12/31/2010. Then compare the ending values. The IUL more than doubled.

The raw S&P index which has no caps on "hoped for" investment gains or any limits on its potential annual losses was virtually flat during those dozen years, while the account value in the IUL (with principal protection) would have safely more than doubled.

Unlike mutual funds, the principal inside of the IUL cannot decrease due to bear markets.

We're getting stock-like positive returns with no downside market risk. You'll notice that all annual gains became protected principal as we go. I only used 7% to illustrate Joseph's policy, although it's likely to do even better than that based on historical data.

There's no way Joseph's CD's could do that good of a job for him nowadays or in the foreseeable future. The "index" interest strategy credited to his IUL has <u>nothing</u> to do with Ben Bernanke, the Federal Reserve or CD rates. And remember that if he died anytime during that period, his wife would get at least $545,000 cash income tax free.

In fact, the tax-free death benefit would likely grow to about $792,000 over the first 20 years (triple his single premium) and keep on growing if he never touched the cash inside of his policy. By moving his cash we'll create almost a $550,000 larger inheritance at that time. The IUL can simultaneously perform many valuable financial functions as well.

If Joseph ever needed or wanted to get some cash out of his policy (whenever he wants) to supplement his income or for a special opportunity, he could easily do that.

Under the same expectations, at age 85 he could take $4,300 out of his policy <u>every month</u> until age 100. That's a total of $750,000 of potential income for himself plus he would still leave a tax-free death benefit of more than the original $250,000 deposit to his spouse or his loved ones. It's a very flexible, safe and tax-deferred emergency fund.

A CD doesn't offer this financial performance or flexibility. Once you understand how to properly use life insurance in this way, it's almost a "no-brainer" for emergency funds. All of these benefits came from a $250,000 single premium he made at age 65, moving some of his money from a low-interest, taxable CD to a "no-market risk" alternative.

We are simply moving money from your left pocket... to your right pocket. It's still all your money, yet we make it work much harder for you without increasing your risks. And you can get access to this "new savings account" for any reason in just a few days if need be. Using an IUL can make every single dollar count – no matter how long you live.

Joseph fully understood the total economic advantages and the multiple *"living benefits"* of turning in his CD early, despite the small penalty. In fact, he easily replaced the small CD penalty he took by the income tax savings in the first 3-6 months alone.

Over time, Joseph will avoid mailing $10,000's to the I.R.S. and Georgia, as well as eliminate thousands more dollars of lost opportunity costs. Those appealing and large-sized tax savings add a lot of value to this financial proposition.

Sally's story...

Sally is a very cautious 72 year old client of mine in Florida. Besides being in great health, she has a nice pension as a retired schoolteacher and also receives her deceased husband's Social Security income. So she has enough monthly cash-flow to fully enjoy her life. That income will last for as long as she lives, so her "savings" are really an emergency fund. She hopes to pass all of those funds on to her children someday.

With about $200,000 in CD's and an annuity she felt that she had plenty of liquid emergency funds yet complained about her CD interest rates that weren't keeping her principal up with inflation -- even ignoring the fact that she had to take money out of her personal checkbook to pay for the taxes on that CD interest income every year.

During and after the last recession she had only earned about 1.5% average interest on her CD's but she had *actually paid* about $4,500 cash to the I.R.S. over the last five years.

This was a "totally unnecessary" transfer of her wealth to the I.R.S. and it was enough money to pay for a couple of nice Alaskan cruises or an unforgettable trip to Europe. She agreed that she's already paying enough taxes to the I.R.S.

She decided to move $100,000 into the IUL and buy the *minimum initial death benefit* of $170,000 allowed by the I.R.S -- keeping $50,000 in CD's and the $93,000 in the annuity.

If Sally doesn't touch the cash value in the policy, as she has no intention of doing, in just ten years her death benefit will grow to $257,000 (assuming an annual average conservative interest crediting of 7.5%). And her legacy won't stop growing there.

By age 87 we expect her policy's initial death benefit to nearly double to $331,000. Those amounts will eventually be left to her three children income tax-free – without any probate, legal costs or months of delay. And those impressive legacy figures should keep on increasing the longer she lives. It's truly a "recession-proof" act of love for her children.

Along with the rising death benefit, her policy's cash surrender value grows too (a more powerful emergency fund – just in case!).

If she ever needs access the cash in her policy for any reason at all, there should be about $182,000 of cash inside the policy at age 84. That's $82,000 of tax-deferred real account growth in just a dozen years... even after deducting all insurance policy fees and expenses. Her cash grew faster than inflation. There's no way that her CD's could ever keep up with any of those figures. Plus her annual income tax bill has gone down too.

So Sally will keep thousands of dollars for her own lifestyle and enjoyment... instead of paying income taxes. If she keeps those saved tax dollars in her own account, it earns interest too (no opportunity costs).

I had *structured all of the above client's policies with three objectives in mind.* Firstly, I wanted to make sure the cash value would grow to combat the very real adverse effects of inflation (without taking market risks or worrying about recessions) in case the client ever needs to access their money for any reason. They can retrieve their cash in just a few days.

Secondly, I wanted them to stop paying unnecessary annual income taxes - taking significant sums of money out of their current lifestyle over time. And lastly, I wanted the death benefit to keep growing as the client lives longer, (along with the cash value) so more income tax-free assets would be quickly passed on to their heirs or charity without any probate costs and delays – (it is totally private with no public records).

What are your own personal financial goals? When seniors know that the money they put into an IUL will *never* be needed by them, since they have substantial other funds and investments, we can structure the policy to provide a much higher initial death benefit. In other cases, we can even make your tax-free legacy much larger still (by 20%-40%) by insuring both the wife and husband in one "second-to-die" survivorship (SIUL) policy which only pays the death benefit after they both have passed away.

A single $1,000,000 premium could produce an immediate tax-free death benefit of perhaps $4,000,000 for a 71 year old couple. An SUIL policy is generally used for estate and legacy planning instead of as a "CD alternative". Yet it can effectively do both jobs well.

We can also use **a properly-designed whole life policy instead which is even more conservative, comes with rock solid guarantees and gives you similar benefits**. However, the overall financial results are less spectacular than portrayed in the above IUL examples.

Which is the right or best way for you to go to completely meet your financial goals?

Each client's circumstances, values and goals are different. It's my job as a planner to match your situation and risk tolerance with the right financial product (solution) and then structure your policy to best achieve your personal financial priorities and wishes.

Let's talk more about this distinct financial tool which offers safety of principal, lots of flexibility, good liquidity and potential double-digit returns -- plus fantastic tax benefits.

And on the next page, I'll also address how using an IUL can increase your current interest income stream so you can enjoy retirement life even more today. You'll see that a properly designed IUL can really help you maintain your purchasing power by giving you potential annual income increases for the rest of your life (recession-proofing your income for life).

First of all, when we use either an IUL or a whole life policy to safely grow your cash savings or to immediately enjoy higher current interest income, we do the exact opposite of what you would do if you were buying life insurance just for the death benefit. It will be counter-intuitive to you, but this *unique policy design process* drives the "asset class" of cash-value life insurance into a brand new realm - offering *multiple living benefits at once.*

So instead of looking for the largest death benefit for the smallest premium, we obtain the <u>least</u> amount of life insurance that the I.R.S. allows, and then put as much cash into our policy as quickly as the I.R.S. will permit us – usually in one single premium payment.

By doing it this way, we have very low insurance expenses inside the policy which gives your policy the best opportunity for impressive growth of both the cash value and the death benefit over time – even at only 6.5%-7.5% average annual interest crediting.

The longer <u>you</u> live… the better your life insurance policy can perform *for you*. I'm assuming that you are going to live a long life, as our life expectancy continues to improve along with constant medical advances. However, should lightning strike or you get hit by a bus, your family or charity will immediately get a death benefit that's substantially more than the amount of money that you deposited into the policy.

No other investments can immediately create and multiply your legacy. It is truly a giving and unselfish act of love for your family. But it is also a smart financial move for your own financial and tax-saving self-interests. It's a win for you and a win for your loved ones.

So far, I've mostly been writing about your cash reserves that are earmarked for "rainy days" and most likely going to be passed on to your loved ones – not money that you need to live on now. You can stop accepting extremely low CD and annuity rates and press your life savings to safely "deliver" more value for you and your family. You can choose to take new, yet prudent steps.

However, if you are looking for additional income 7-9 years from now (or perhaps you are expecting an inheritance or a sale of a property), we can simply structure your policy differently to give you ***reliable tax-free income* in the future**. That's right… tax-free income.

First, let's discuss how an IUL can help you get more income right away (taxable) with planned annual income increases… to better enjoy your retirement for years to come. An IUL can be a perfect interest "income producer" right now and it is often a much more attractive financial vehicle than an annuity, CD or bond portfolio when one wants higher income today (that should even grow each year) – without taking market risks.

Do you want higher interest income <u>right now</u>?

John is a 74 year old who lives in California and is enjoying excellent health, along with his wife Susan. They expect to live a long time. He had an old 5 year annuity with a cash surrender value of $300,000. He had owned this annuity for over 4 years and it pays him a fixed 4% interest rate now… yet John knew that rate wouldn't last for much longer. The insurance company was paying him the earned interest on a quarterly basis.

John had originally come to me for help with his brokerage accounts. My fee-based advisory (RIA) firm manages his son's I.R.A., and Tom had suggested he learn about the high-quality third party money managers that I often use to manage my client's portfolios.

These private wealth managers were carefully chosen after passing rigorous "risk and performance screens" - low volatility in the very bad years and good returns in the rest.

All of these private money managers *broke even or actually made money* during the last two recessions and bear markets (2000-2002 and 2008) and averaged at least 7% annualized returns since 2000 (net of all fees). In a nutshell, they have far out-performed the S&P 500 with less than half of the risk and price volatility over the last dozen years. I'll discuss these money managers further in a later chapter.

In the course of our phone conversations John had also expressed concern that when the 5 year annuity's term was over, that he would <u>not</u> be able to find another 4% interest rate. He did not want his interest income to drop. Since they mostly depend upon a fixed income, increasing costs of living in the future was also a big worry of theirs.

So in addition to my now managing John's large I.R.A. with four of my select low-risk money managers, we settled on moving his $300,000 annuity money into an IUL right away. With John's great health, the minimum (I.R.S.) initial death benefit was $463,000.

Using a "depression-era" <u>ultra</u>-conservative 6.65% crediting rate (which was the actual <u>lowest</u> crediting rate in <u>any</u> 15 year period since 1930), the insurance company will make a monthly deposit into his bank account with a 4% interest rate for the remainder of his life. When he passes away, Susan will be further protected by the fact that she will get a substantially larger tax-free death benefit than the annuity would have ever provided.

But I made it even better for them. I set it up so that his interest income may rise by 3% each year for the rest of his life to fight the effects of inflation. So every year their monthly deposit should get larger by 3%. In all likelihood, his IUL will be able to deliver even more income than this. Will your annuity, CD or bond portfolio do that for you?

Dottie is a very conservative 67 year old new client in "pretty good" health. She was unhappy with her $85,000 CD that was earning less than 1% or just $750 *per year*. When I told her that I could *quadruple* her interest income... plus leave her son more than the $85,000 when she passes away, she was "all ears" -- as long as it didn't involve taking risks.

She was delighted that her IUL would safely pay her over $308 *per month* to start out ($3,400 per year). For some people this amount isn't much, but it did improve *her* lifestyle. So we simply moved the CD money (taking a small penalty) and then re-positioned the cash into an IUL.

Not only was she able to enjoy *four times* as much interest income right away, but I set the policy up so that her recession-proof interest income should rise by 3% every year for the rest of her life (using a very conservative 6.85% average annual return).

That tax-free death benefit is nearly $18,000 more money than the CD value would have been for her son. At age 92, her interest income should grow to $6,750 per year.

If getting more current income isn't important now, you may be concerned about paying for the high cost of potential long-term care (LTC) expenses someday. There are other types of life insurance policies that will not only give your loved ones a death benefit, they are also guaranteed to multiply your single premium by 3-5 times to pay for home care or other LTC benefits on a _tax-free_ basis – with NO out-of-pocket annual premiums.

So you can rely on guaranteed Long-Term Care benefits if you need them... or give your loved ones the death benefit if you don't. Some of these LTC-life insurance "hybrid" policies also offer a full 100% lifetime money-back guarantee should you ever change your mind. Again, we can make your some of your life savings perform multiple duties for you.

How "index" interest is credited to your IUL policy

My financial practice is all about the "preservation of capital" and reducing risks. I've written about average annual "index" crediting rates of 7%-8% (up to 12%-14% in the good years) and in this low interest rate environment you're right to ask yourself, how can an IUL do that? Looking at actual annual returns data over the last dozen years and even back-testing all the way back as far as 1930 – they do. It's a historical fact.

If you _can totally_ **eliminate EVERY single negative year** _in the stock market_, doesn't an average annual return of 7% or more over many years make perfectly good sense to you?

Although there are slight differences between how the "index interest" strategies in different IUL policies operate, most function in a similar way. The interest credited to your policy is "TIED" to a market index - usually the S&P 500 index, over a 12 month period.

The S&P 500 index comprises the 500 largest public companies in the USA – Coke, Boeing, GE, Home Depot, Disney, IBM, AT&T, Exxon, Walmart, Visa, McDonald's, Google, Apple, UPS, Proctor & Gamble, 3M, Starbucks, Microsoft, Target, Goldman Sachs, Intel, Pfizer, etc.

Let's be clear, that even though the interest credited to your contract is "tied" to how well the S&P 500 index performs (excluding dividends), your money is never actually invested in the stock market, which is why it is never at risk in bear markets or recessions. That's very important – **_your money in an IUL is never invested in the stock market_**.

Most IUL policies have a "floor" and a "cap" on the "indexed" interest rate your policy's account will be credited with each year, subject to how well the S&P index does.

Depending upon the specific IUL policy you choose, the "floor" is between 0% and 1%. The "floor" means this is the _least amount of interest_ that your contract will be credited with in any one policy year (unless you choose the fixed rate - now at 3.95%). My favorite IUL has a "_worst case_" index floor rate of 1% which is pretty attractive. A 1% rate is very comparable to current taxable CD rates... that have no upside or extra death benefit at all.

In years like 2008 where there was a huge drop in the S&P 500 index, many of my IUL clients proudly told me that "zero was their hero". In other words, even a zero (or a +2%) percent return was awesome compared to the huge -37% loss in the S&P 500 index.

After avoiding all of the market losses in 2008, all IUL policies that I use were credited 12%-14% (up to the caps) in 2009 and 2010. That's pretty impressive. The main thing to understand is that your cash account value can never decrease because the stock market goes down.

You safely avoid all losses because your policy's cash value is never actually invested in stocks or mutual funds. Look at the historical S&P 500 index and IUL returns below.

	Year	S&P 500 Index	IUL Index Allocation	Fixed Interest Rate
NO Negative Years... Ever	1987	2.0%	2.00%	5.0%
	1988	12.4%	12.40%	5.0%
	1989	27.3%	14.00%	5.0%
	1990	-6.6%	0.00%	5.0%
	1991	26.3%	14.00%	5.0%
+7.76%	1992	4.5%	4.50%	5.0%
	1993	7.1%	7.10%	5.0%
	1994	-1.5%	0.00%	5.0%
25 Year Average Return	1995	34.1%	14.00%	5.0%
	1996	20.3%	14.00%	5.0%
	1997	31.0%	14.00%	5.0%
	1998	26.7%	14.00%	5.0%
	1999	19.5%	14.00%	5.0%
	2000	-10.1%	0.00%	5.0%
	2001	-13.0%	0.00%	5.0%
	2002	-23.4%	0.00%	5.0%
	2003	26.4%	14.00%	5.0%
	2004	9.0%	9.00%	5.0%
	2005	3.0%	3.00%	5.0%
	2006	13.6%	13.60%	5.0%
	2007	3.5%	3.50%	5.0%
	2008	-37%	0.00%	4.0%
	2009	23.5%	14.00%	4.0%
Annual Point to Point Average 0% floor and 14% cap	2010	12.8%	12.80%	4.0%
	2011	0.00%	0.00%	4.0%

**13 out of 25 years the IUL had double-digit returns of 12.4% or better
with NO NEGATIVE YEARS... EVER!**

Now let's talk about the "cap". In years where the S&P 500 does extremely well, your policy will be credited by an interest rate that is "limited" by a cap which is generally between 12%-14% a year. So if the actual S&P 500 index goes up by 20% one year, the maximum interest rate credited to your account is limited by your policy's cap.

But unlike the actual S&P 500 index, your annual interest gains are always locked-in and can NEVER be lost by market drops in the future. This is a considerable advantage for you. That's right. Your annual interest gains become "protected principal" and are never at risk when the market goes down again... which it eventually will. And there is always the fixed interest rate option (currently 3.95%) instead of using the index strategy.

Some people may see caps as a negative, but if you never have to "make-up" for bear market losses and your past interest gains are protected forever, it's really tough to beat these products' performance over the long-term.

In fact, an IUL policy with a 1% floor and a 13% cap would have substantially beat the raw S&P 500 index that had no caps on its gains, nor any limits on its annual losses, in many "rolling 15 year investment periods" going back from the depression years through 2011 – with no capital losses in any one year.

How does it all work? The insurance company <u>uses ONLY the interest they earn</u> from your premium (never your principal) to buy a "call option spread" on the S&P 500 index. If the index goes down, the options simply expire worthless and you get no return that year.

If the index goes up, the call option spread makes a profit, and your account is credited with the full gain on the option (up to the cap). So your principal is never at risk. The worst thing that can happen is getting a zero % (or +1%) return.

Your worst years are 0-1% and your best are up to 12%-14% (averaging about 7%-8% per year). When you combine the insurance company using only the interest they earn from your principal to buy principal risk-free options with the "reset" (described below), you get potential growth without risk.

Want to take even less risk… but get less reward? Okay, let's look at a specially-designed whole life policy instead. Designed properly, either product can handily beat a bank CD. Wouldn't you sleep well at night knowing that your emergency fund can never lose money when the market goes down… and yet you can enjoy up to double-digit gains when the market goes up to beat the consequences of long-term inflation in the years?

And until you take money out of your life insurance policy, it's all tax-deferred so you don't pay any income taxes on your interest either. So your interest earns interest. Is this something that you might be interested in learning more about? And it gets even better.

Of course, you can get the same protection from loss of principal if you invest in CD's and fixed annuities but you generally do not get the potential of earning up to 12%-14%. Unlike life insurance, interest in those investments is generally taxed either each and every year… or at death.

A tax is <u>always</u> paid or owed in the future on CD's, bonds and annuities. With a life policy you can completely avoid both current… *and even future taxation*.

Bear in mind that CD's, bonds mutual funds and most annuities have no extra death benefit. That's a very important and significant added monetary value for your family.

The annual "locking-in and reset" is pure genius

If a 0-1% "indexed" annual floor interest rate (completely avoiding all market losses) and the potential for 12%-14% annual gains aren't already attractive enough, here's an additional benefit of the IUL that's pure genius over stocks, ETF's and mutual funds in how it can safely grow your cash reserves or current income. It's the annual index "reset".

The power of the index reset mechanism is that **you can actually grow your principal when the index rebounds after big market drops -- while stock, mutual fund and variable annuity investors are waiting, hoping and praying... just to breakeven again**. The chart on the next page compares an IUL (1% floor/13% cap) to an S&P 500 fund and how the index reset takes a $33,143 advantage of market rebounds (excluding fees and expenses on both).

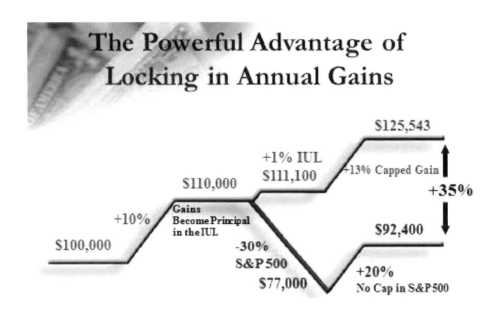

That is a $33,143 POSITIVE difference because of the annual lock-in and reset in just 3 years. S&P index fund is in RED and the IUL is in GREEN.

Compare investing in an S&P 500 index fund... to an IUL

What about the money you have in mutual funds, Exchange Traded Funds (ETF's) and stocks? You probably keep it there so you can hopefully get a good return on it someday. Maybe they are paying good dividends and are worth holding on to if you don't mind the large risk of the loss of your capital. But are the risks of the stock market, mutual funds and the like getting to be more than you can... or should bear? Like most folks, you want the potential for double-digit positive returns yet you don't want to lose any principal.

With the market drops of 2000, 2001 and 2002 and again in 2008 – are your mutual funds, ETF's and stocks still trying to get back to where they were back in 1999? An IUL protects all of your past gains and even allows your savings to grow in market rebounds.

Bob is a healthy 67 year old who had taken a "gamble" by investing $100,000 lump sum in a low-cost S&P 500 index fund on January 1st, 1999. If we use the actual historical annual returns of that index (excluding dividends and fund expenses) his account would only be worth $103,000 on Dec. 31st, 2011. That's a pitiful gain of only $3,000 over 13 full years. He would have had little growth in his index mutual fund over those 4,745 *days*.

Could that happen again? You bet it could. Gosh, it actually took the DOW (DJIA) until 1954 just to reach its 1929 high again. That was waiting 25 long years -- to just breakeven.

However, if Bob had the same $100,000 safely sitting in his IUL contract on January 1st, 1999 with an initial income tax-free death benefit of $200,000, the actual net CASH SURRENDER VALUE in his policy would have grown to about $188,000 by the end of 2011.

And he would have had no stress or sleepless nights along the way. And his wife was also very comforted by the much larger death benefit... just in case. That's peace of mind.

There is $188,000 in cash account value – even AFTER deducting all of the insurance policy loads, costs, fees and charges with the actual 7% annual crediting rate over that time with a 2% percent floor and a cap of only 12%. That's an impressive difference of over $85,000 dollars in favor of the IUL due to the safety of the 1% floor (no market losses ever), locking-in past gains and the annual reset mechanism over that awful thirteen year period.

Stock market surges can be very exciting... but steep market drops can erase years of gains. You don't need to *sit out* to stay above water. Even during 1930-1954 where investors were still waiting to breakeven from 1929, an IUL would have credited over 7% average annual interest, because there were a number of "up" years during that period.

In fact, the "worst" 25 year investment period on record since 1930 still had a 7.11% average annual interest rate with those caps and floors. And the **average annual return during all "15, 20 & 25 year investment periods" from 1930-2011 was 7.65%.** It's a very safe way to stay well ahead of inflation over time -- without market risk to your principal.

And what if the S&P 500 index had gone up by 20% in 2011? Would Bob prefer the "ending account balance" after a 12% capped gain on $188,000... or after getting the full 20% gain on only 103,000? The answer is perfectly clear. Plus the future performance of the stock market can never take those past gains away, since they are now locked-in and have become protected principal. That's very compelling. To most folks that's real security.

Additionally, if Bob had died *anytime* during that period, his wife or loved ones would get at least $200,000 dollars income tax free. In fact, the death benefit should gradually grow to about $315,000 by the end of 20 years and will keep growing if he never touches the policy's cash value. Who knows what the value of the stock market would be then?

However, if he ever did take some income distributions (for any reason) from his single-premium policy, the earned interest would be taxable just like interest income from bonds, annuities, CD's or mutual funds. There's absolutely no way those investment alternatives could give all of these valuable advantages and predictability for himself and his family.

But wait... if enjoying tax-free income sometime in the future is more important to you than taking immediate income or growing your future legacy for your loved ones, we would structure the policy differently. Instead of making a single $100,000 lump sum premium payment into the contract, we would just make five annual deposits of $20,000.

Simply by following longstanding I.R.S. codes 7702 and 72(e), we can ensure that any income that you take from your IUL or whole life policy would be 100% income tax free -- with many more financial benefits than owning muni bonds.

And that tax-free income would not cause your Social Security checks to be taxed or put you into a higher tax bracket. There's no way that your CD's, mutual funds or annuities can be tax-free unless they're in a ROTH IRA. And a ROTH doesn't have a big death benefit.

Yet any properly structured life insurance contract has been able to do that since 1913 including the tax code modifications made in the 1980's – as long as you follow the straightforward I.R.S. rules. In many cases, this is so much more attractive than tax-free muni-bonds. If you are feeling a little confused – don't worry. So just contact me so we can fully discuss this.

So if enjoying an immediate income stream and/or owning a secure and fast growing emergency fund while instantly increasing your legacy is your main goal, we simply make a single premium payment. However, if enjoying a *monthly tax-free income stream at some point in the future* is more important to you, we would simply structure the "planned premium payment" to be deposited into your policy over a period of 4, 5, 6 or 7 years.

Examples of using a whole life policy

Many readers will be anxious to see how well an IUL policy will meet their needs as a strong CD, bond or annuity substitute. Others may also want to compare how a whole life policy might look for them. And this isn't your "father's" whole life policy. It's one based on the latest CSO mortality costs with a unique purpose-built structure to be a flexible, safe alternative place to keep your "emergency" cash – with multiple financial benefits.

The following chart shows an example of a 60 year old female in excellent health and compares this option to her other financial alternatives. She makes a one-time $120,000 premium deposit resulting in an immediate $306,000 (and ever-rising) death benefit.

As shown in earlier client examples, this whole life policy is really designed to grow the cash value for potential future needs. The huge and ever-growing tax-free legacy "comes along for the ride" if she never touches the policy's cash account value.

In the first few years, the whole life policy may not look quite as appealing as the alternatives on the right. But that's _only_ if you ignore the very large tax-free death benefit.

Flexible Choice Whole Life   Other Alternatives

| Year | Age | Premium Outlay | Non-Guaranteed Values at Illustrated Dividend Scale[1] | | Non-Guaranteed After-Tax Values[3] | | |
			Total Cash Value[2]	Total Death Benefit	Certificate of Deposit[4] (1.71%)	Taxable Bond[5] (4.63%)	Tax-Exempt Bond[5] (3.35%)
1	61	$ 120,000	$ 112,934	$ 306,267	$ 121,477	$ 124,000	$ 124,020
5	65	-	$ 137,949	$ 322,190	$ 127,571	$ 141,380	$ 141,493
10	70	-	$ 179,013	$ 317,827	$ 135,620	$ 166,570	$ 166,835
15	75	-	$ 233,184	$ 365,028	$ 144,177	$ 196,248	$ 196,715
20	80	-	$ 301,483	$ 422,162	$ 153,274	$ 231,213	$ 231,948
25	85	-	$ 385,943	$ 490,972	$ 162,945	$ 272,408	$ 273,491
30	90	-	$ 484,640	$ 572,752	$ 173,226	$ 320,943	$ 322,475
35	95	-	$ 597,317	$ 664,764	$ 184,156	$ 378,125	$ 380,232
40	100	-	$ 721,246	$ 772,742	$ 195,775	$ 445,496	$ 448,333
45	105	-	$ 863,807	$ 896,596	$ 208,127	$ 524,870	$ 528,631
50	110	-	$ 1,019,457	$ 1,036,044	$ 221,259	$ 618,385	$ 623,312
55	115	-	$ 1,191,133	$ 1,194,130	$ 235,219	$ 728,563	$ 734,950
60	120	-	$ 1,385,378	$ 1,373,906	$ 250,060	$ 858,370	$ 866,583

[1] Illustrated at the current dividend scale or lower. For the dividend option selected, please see the full basic illustration for the life insurance policy described. Dividends are neither guarantees nor estimates of future results.

That large death benefit would be left to her loved ones from day one. That's an immediate and considerable financial advantage that the other options can never match.

After just 5-7 years the policy's cash value looks so much more attractive. And then compare the values at ages 75, 80, 85 and 90. There's no comparison whatsoever at those ages. The whole life policy above looks great, yet an IUL would be even more compelling with the potential for double-digit interest gains and even lower current mortality costs.

Roger was 69 when he asked me about better alternatives for $150,000 sitting in a CD that was about to renew at only 1.85%. He realized that level of interest wasn't even going to keep pace with inflation (which he believed was actually much higher than the "official" government CPI rates). He wasn't spending the interest and had no intention of using it.

Like so many other retirees, he was paying the yearly tax on the CD interest out of his checkbook. He could afford to pay the annual taxes now, although he had much better ideas for other uses of his tax savings than sending those dollars to the I.R.S. He felt very comfortable with how I used a uniquely designed whole life policy for him, so he simply re-positioned those funds into the single premium policy.

The initial death benefit for his wife Patty was be $317,000. This made her feel much more comfortable than only having $150,000 at the bank. He likes the yearly tax savings and the reliable growth of his cash.

Based on current dividends, and making no further premium payments, the cash value in his policy should grow, without any taxation, to over $200,000 within 10 years. At age 85, there should be some $270,000 cash value in this multi-purpose "emergency account".

By age 90, we expect the cash value to have swelled to nearly $340,000 and the tax-free death benefit would escalate to $365,000 and continue to climb. He is enjoying a very competitive internal rate of return on his cash reserves to safely fight inflation, has lowered his annual income tax bill, avoided all opportunity costs, and greatly increased his legacy from day one.

It's a very well balanced and effective financial solution. He still often tells me that, **"it's one of the smartest financial moves I've ever made"**.

In my practice, more and more seniors are becoming very comfortable with IUL's, yet there is absolutely nothing wrong with buying a tried and true *new* whole life policy. A whole life policy's cash value and death benefit aren't affected at all by the roller-coaster ride on Wall Street.

As long as a whole life policy is primarily designed to be a CD substitute by minimizing the initial death benefit to the lowest amount possible (per I.R.S. rules) and using other proven yet seldom used "tricks of the trade", it will perform very well for you.

Again, it all comes down to planning for your personal circumstances and financial goals. Either way, under most circumstances, it will be almost impossible for CD's, money market funds or bonds to equal a purpose-built life policy. Whole life insurance is more conservative and IUL's safely offer much more upside. Speaking of bonds and bond funds, don't forget that the bonds prices usually go down in value when interest rates go up.

This is NOT an indexed annuity!

Please don't confuse an IUL policy to "fixed indexed annuities" that many insurance agents are selling to seniors as a safe investment. Like an IUL, a fixed indexed annuity is a safe investment because your principal can never go lower due to losses in the stock market and your past gains always become protected principal.

However, most annuity sales people have absolutely no idea that in many cases, an IUL policy will do a much better job of meeting more of your financial intentions and goals with even more flexibility.

I sometimes recommend annuities too... when they are the "right fit" for the client. Since an I.R.A. cannot own a life insurance policy, I usually reserve fixed or indexed annuities for I.R.A. money when they are absolutely unwilling to take ANY market risks and understand the trade-offs to their lifestyle and/or legacy.

Sometimes I use other non-qualified (non-IRA) annuities to be bought for a specific financial purpose such as to provide for future long-term care benefits or to take advantage of tax-deferral with our 3rd party money managers which I'll discuss later on. But in 75%-85% of the time, when a well-informed client actually makes a side-by-side comparison between purchasing a brand new "indexed or fixed annuity"... to a new single-premium insurance contract, the client will usually choose the IUL or whole life policy over the annuity. And that can be true even if you would like to spend your interest income now (as I showed you in some client examples earlier in this report). How can that be?

Even though both products use the same "call option spreads" to credit index interest, the interest index "caps" are usually *two to five times higher* in an IUL than they are with index annuities. So both your IUL cash account value and your death benefit can grow about twice as fast to fight inflation. However, the principal protection, tax-deferral, the annual "reset" and the locking-in of all past index interest gains work the same in both.

And of course, the death benefit of any life insurance policy is always income tax free - while every dollar of retained earnings in the annuity will always be taxed at death. This is important if you think income tax rates will be rising -- *because someone will pay taxes*.

Unlike non-qualified annuities, **if we design your life policy to comply with I.R.S. code 7702, you can actually enjoy *tax-free* income at some point in the future**. Maybe you are expecting an inheritance later -- we can set-up the policy now to provide you with tax-free income from that lump sum. That's pretty impressive financial, estate and tax planning.

If you do own an annuity, you might like to compare the newest available "models" with what you own. Some offer compelling guaranteed streams of income for your lifetime (or even for joint lives) without giving up the control of and access to your principal. These might be attractive to some people for I.R.A. accounts but think twice about it and take a close look at other alternatives.

One tax-deferred variable annuity (VA) allows us to invest with the same low-risk 3rd party wealth managers (described later in the book) and let them manage your money rather than use riskier mutual funds.

This annuity has *no-surrender charges* (it's 100% liquid). And it *only costs $20 per month (no matter how much is invested)* instead of the typically high fees of 1.0%-1.4% of your account value each year. That saves my clients $1,000's annually. It's fully tax-deferred and has a great long-term track record of good returns and low volatility.

A Long-Term Care insurance alternative

Traditional LTC insurance policies can be very expensive to own and premiums do go up. So some annuities are guaranteed to immediately "triple" your principal, should you need to pay for future long-term care (LTC) expenses. With LTC costs currently running at some $4,000-$7,000 per month, they are expected to nearly double in just 15-20 years.

These special annuities qualifying under the Pension Protection Act (PPA) can pay out cash for future and unpredictable LTC expenses – *without any income taxation* on your past gains.

Do you remember Sally from earlier in the book and her $93,000 non-qualified annuity? Over many years, her annuity had built-up some $42,000 of tax-deferred gains inside of that contract. She didn't realize she would have to (and then didn't want to) pay taxes on the gains if she needed to access that money to pay for long-term care expenses.

So we simply moved that $93,000 annuity to a brand new type of LTC annuity that fully conforms to the Pension Protection Act (PPA) by using a 1035 tax-free exchange. It was very **easy to help her avoid paying those deferred income taxes should she ever need to pay for LTC expenses, while instantly tripling her "funds for LTC" from day one**. That's smart income tax planning combined with supplying substantial extra LTC cash benefits.

Her new special no-exam annuity "triples" the amount in the policy (for LTC costs only) should she ever need long-term care (LTC) in her home, an assisted living facility or even in a nursing home. If she needs LTC in the future, she can use up to $279,000 in that annuity to pay for her LTC expenses (instead of only the $93,000 including a $42,000 taxable gain).

If Sally uses money from that particular annuity for any qualified LTC services, she does *not* have to pay any income taxes on her withdrawals. That's a pretty attractive deal. If she never needs LTC, then she still owns, fully controls and can bequeath the annuity. She has had no expensive out-of-pocket traditional long-term care insurance premium to pay either. Plus there's less rigorous medical underwriting to get approved for LTC coverage.

Let's look at what annuities you currently own and then compare possible alternatives that may better meet your present needs and/or your new financial goals.

Life insurance loads, fees and expenses

Your banker, stockbroker, advisor, friend or know-it-all neighbor will tell you that life insurance policies have expensive loads, fees and charges and that's very true... **BUT <u>ONLY</u> IF the policy is <u>not</u> structured properly and fully-funded** to safely maximize the growth of your cash value by *only using the minimum initial death benefit allowed by the I.R.S. rules.*

Each and every life insurance policy absolutely needs to be designed and built for a specific financial purpose by someone who really knows what they are doing and who is only looking out for <u>your</u> best interests -- as you have been shown in prior examples.

Contrary to popular yet inaccurate public opinion, all of the benefits of a properly-designed IUL policy will only cost about 1% a year in expenses and fees over the long-term. That's about the same cost of what most equity mutual fund managers charge you to under-perform the stock market year after year.

A fully-funded IUL contract on the life of a "senior" should provide an actual *tax-deferred* "cash-on-cash" net internal rate of return (I.R.R.) of between 4.5% - 6% over the long-term. That net return figure is <u>after</u> all insurance loads, fees and expenses have been deducted. That's a safe, very liquid, tax-deferred I.R.R. with a big death benefit to boot.

Depending upon your I.R.S. and state tax bracket you would need to earn a *"pre-tax equivalent"* return of 6%-9% a year to equal that. Most retirees would be very happy with that level of safe return. Plus the internal rate of return on the tax-free death benefit is even higher.

Since we are all going to pass away someday, at least the tax-free death benefit gives you something of value for your 1% or so of long-term annual policy expenses. Over a long period, most mutual fund managers can't honestly say they add any extra value over an index fund -- yet they still deduct their fees from your account each and every single year.

Do you already own cash-value life insurance?

In fact, you may have a whole life or some type of universal life insurance policy in force already. Even though you are older now, it sometimes makes absolute financial sense to do a tax-free exchange (1035X) from the old kinds of policies to a new one which has lower mortality costs due to the fact that we are living longer than decades ago.

For some strange reason, life insurance is the only industry that tries to keep people from "trading in" their obsolete products for a newer, improved version. Maybe it's time for an upgrade.

The internal insurance costs in all life insurance policies are largely determined by the CSO mortality table used. But over the years as our longevity has increased, these mortality tables have changed – getting a lot less expensive (by 30% to 50% or more).

A new IUL (or even a new whole life policy) can have much less expensive internal mortality costs (using the latest and least expensive CSO life expectancy tables due to increasing longevity in the USA) even though you are older now.

The bottom line is that your current life policy is likely costing you too much, even if your annual premiums are being paid out of the policy cash values or dividends. **You can possibly get a much larger death benefit, stop future premium payments… or get a new policy with enhanced tax-free Long-Term Care benefits at no out-of-pocket cost to you**.

Plus you can enjoy opportunities to safely earn up to 12%-14%. The average annual IUL interest credited over the last 25 years would have been +7.9%. In fact, the average annual returns during "ANY 15 or 20 or 25 or 30 year period" since 1930 were all over +7.61%. That's pretty impressive considering there is no stock market risk.

Why settle for a low fixed interest rate return when you can have the opportunity to get both a fixed interest rate or an index strategy (or a combination of the two).

We just need to carefully analyze your old policy and see what may be best for you now. Based on my many years of experience, you'll very likely be very pleased with the policy analysis and your options to make a substantial improvement.

Let's make sure that any of your existing life policies are pulling their own weight and that your family would not be better served with a brand new one. My team does in-depth life insurance "audits" every month for seniors at no cost and without any obligation.

Those Pesky Required Minimum Distributions (RMD's)

Here's another effective use of an IUL that your stockbroker or financial advisor probably hasn't suggested to you, if you are one of millions of retirees that have I.R.A.'s that they do not need or want to take Required Minimum Distributions starting at age 70½.

If you do not need the income from these required annual distributions (RMD's) from your I.R.A. what can you do with that required and unnecessary, but taxable income?

Well here's what Tom and Dana are doing with one of their I.R.A.'s that is worth $110,000 now. Even though neither of them are age 70½ yet (Tom is age 66 and Dana is 68), they want to take advantage of their good health and get started with this powerful tax-free wealth transference strategy.

Right now this I.R.A. is invested in an annuity paying 5% (guaranteed for life) which is an annual income of $5,500 that they will have to pay taxes on. They bought this new annuity from me as part of this planned legacy enhancement strategy. Since their current total tax rate is 30%, they will owe taxes to the I.R.S. and their state of $1,650. That leaves them with a net of $3,850 each year that they do not need to maintain their current lifestyle.

With that $3,850 guaranteed lifetime income stream (this is NOT annuitization so we could still have control and access to the I.R.A. principal if needed) we bought a survivorship IUL policy. The SUIL has an initial death benefit (after the second spouse passes away) of $200,000 that should actually grow over time. Using that $3,850 annual premium and a conservative interest crediting rate of 7% average, in 20 years the death benefit will actually rise to over $296,000 tax-free for their grandchildren.

So we took an unneeded and taxable $110,000 I.R.A. with an after-tax value of some $99,000 (if the grandchildren are only in the 10% tax bracket when they both pass)... and we are slowly withdrawing funds (which they would have to do at age 70½ anyway), to more than double (and eventually nearly triple) the after-tax gift to their beloved grandchildren. Of course any funds left inside the I.R.A. will pass to the grandkids as well.

And along the way, if they ever need access to more funds, they still have whatever principal is still left inside of the I.R.A. annuity plus there should be nearly $100,000 in 20 years (which can be accessed tax-free) inside of their SIUL.

So what is the catch?

Double-digit potential annual gains to combat long-term inflation; no market risk to your principal during recessions and it immediately increases your legacy to protect your spouse or provide for your family. It's always tax-deferred (saving you $1,000's of tax dollars now)... and it can even be totally tax-free. By now you are probably asking yourself what's the catch? Why haven't you heard of these single-premium IUL plans before?

Even though **brand new IUL policy sales are on track to reach over $1.3 BILLION dollars of premiums this year**, most insurance agents, bankers, investment advisors and stockbrokers have no idea how these policies work, have never used them, nor know how to structure them properly to give you the most potent "living" benefits and flexibility.

But utilizing quality IUL's for immediately _increasing_ income streams for retirees right now (and raising their income in the future), safely growing emergency funds, providing future tax-free retirement income (like a ROTH IRA), estate and charitable planning, college funding and other important financial goals has been a specialty of mine since 2004. It was then that I realized that there was not a more formidable, multi-purpose and fully flexible, yet very conservative financial planning vehicle, than a properly-structured IUL contract.

Or we can effectively use a specially-designed, quality whole life policy which has very low correlation to other asset classes. Most agents do not use the same powerful whole life policy "structures" to make them perform as a very potent cash, CD or bond substitute.

As you've seen, an IUL can significantly increase your retirement interest income right now, years in the future… or just dramatically enhance your legacy from day one. It offers a great deal of flexibility for any unforeseen changes in your future financial needs.

Retirement is a three decade long challenge -- one that you cannot afford to lose. No stockbroker, banker or any money manager can guarantee against loss of principal, yet still offer you 12%-14% potential returns that get "locked-in" and protected each year. And except for ROTH's or muni bonds, they cannot offer you the potential for tax-free income or a tax-free legacy either.

But life insurance and annuities are <u>only</u> financial "tools". Just like a carpenter, I use the right tools to meet a specific financial need or goal. Financial planning is solving tough financial problems and challenges or improving circumstances by using the right "tools" in the right way.

Much Better Investment Options for I.R.A.'s

You may know that an I.R.A. cannot own a life insurance policy as an investment (nor collectibles, stamps, antiques, artwork, or wine collections, etc.). So as much as many of my clients would like to put some of their I.R.A. money into an IUL or whole life policy it can't be done — without taking a taxable distribution and then paying income taxes on that money first.

So these clients often look to other safe places to "recession-proof" their I.R.A. funds. For some retirees, it's a fixed annuity that operates like a long-term CD. Others prefer the "index" annuities that I mentioned earlier in the report with "guaranteed lifetime income riders". Although they both types of annuities can be better than CD's right now, both options offer pitiful interest rates and present little protection against inflation since they are not "built" to regularly increase your income. But they might be a "partial" solution for you depending upon your own financial goals and unique circumstances.

Others choose variable annuities with "guaranteed income riders" that offer guaranteed minimum lifetime income benefits -- no matter how badly the world stock and bond markets do. Variable annuities have sub-accounts inside of them which are very similar to mutual funds – and carry all the same ups and downs. These income riders can be appealing but they come with *very high fees*. In a bull market, there's more upside potential for capital and income growth… but with a lot more risk to your principal in a bad or long bear market.

And if one ever needs complete access to their money in a lump sum from a variable annuity, the account values have absolutely no limits on its potential losses. You could be shocked at your actual account or death benefit after a brutal recession – especially after taking years of income distributions. In most cases, I *would not count on* much income inflation protection either.

But there is another relatively safe option for I.R.A. money that you can't afford to take big losses on, but need to re-grow its value to combat inflation through your likely longevity (or your taxable brokerage accounts and even any annuities with large tax-deferred gains too).

Earlier I wrote about some of the third party institutional money managers that we work with that **performed very well during the last two recessions with much lower risk** than the S&P 500. They actually had *positive* stock market-like returns with low volatility (only small and brief capital losses) -- which can help you reach your lifetime "rising income" goals.

These investments are kept at the Trust Company of America (TCA), where hundreds of large and small fee-based Registered Investment Advisory firms have managed custodial accounts since 1972. TCA faithfully serves over 105,000 client accounts and has $11 Billion dollars in client assets there – trusts, pension funds, 401(k)'s, I.R.A.'s, endowments, etc.

Each of these proven money managers uses different strategies to reduce volatility and principal risk. The least "risky" of these strategies had 86% LESS volatility than the S&P 500. The "most aggressive" strategy… still had less than half of the S&P 500's volatility.

Amongst the four investment strategies, the LOWEST 3 year, 5 year and 10 year average annual returns were +8.95%, +8.8% and +7.93% respectively (**All stated returns are NET of ALL investment fees**).

In fact, the manager with the "worst" 1-year return during the last decade only lost -4.65% (2008) and then came back and earned an average of 14% annual returns over the next three years (2009-2011).

Conversely, the highest 3, 5 and 10 year annual returns were 20.1%, 14.68% and 13.4% respectively. That compares to 23.3%, 1.93% and just 4.1% for the far riskier S&P 500 index. None of our money managers use the old, failed: "buy, hold… and keep praying" approach.

Our fee-based advisory group has some $200 million invested with these four managers and as a group we are adding some $10 million a month of investor funds to these proven money managers.

Rather than choose between these four different investment strategies, I typically recommend that my clients invest some amounts in each so can enjoy an even "smoother ride"-- **while still taking 68% less risk than in the S&P 500**. This combined manager approach actually earned a positive 3.1% interest in 2008 while the S&P 500 dropped a whopping -37% that year.

An equally weighted portfolio earned 15.3%, 10.98% and 10.3% over the last 3, 5 and 10 years respectively, with only minor "potholes". I focus on safety -- not hoping for big returns.

I've highlighted taking income from just one of the strategies available to clients of my firm below. This institutional money manager began this powerful strategy in April 2001 (now with **SEVEN BILLION dollars of assets under their management** – from pension funds, etc.).

The graph shows how starting with $1,000,000, a client could have enjoyed 6% annual distributions ($60,000 per year) and even increased those distributions by 3% each year (now at $76,000 per year) – even through two U.S. recessions. A remarkable $753,000 was distributed as income over that period of time.

After taking all of those income withdrawals, by the end of 2011, there was still nearly $1,400,000 dollars in the account compared to only $481,000 in an alternative investment in an unmanaged, but "low-cost" S&P 500 index fund.

A big loss one could never recover from! This manager's ending balance had a positive growth of nearly +40% ... compared to a painful loss of over -52% in the index fund. In actual dollars and cents, that's a big difference of $912,000 "real dollars" in less than eleven years.

The BLUE line is the money manager and the RED line is the S&P 500. The lines show investment performance combined with the income withdrawals. When the S&P lost -22% in 2002 and -37% in 2008, this manager gained +2.55% in 2002 and only lost -4.65% in 2008.

To be fair, the S&P 500 did beat this particular money manager by +6.5% in 2003 and by less than +3% in the years 2005, 2006 and 2011. But were those minor wins worth the risks of the big losses in 2002 and 2008?

How did your own mutual funds perform over this period? If you are like most people, your investments didn't fare as well. If so, can you afford continuing with their likely poor performance?

How could this investment manager perform this well? They were able to do that by being able to go to cash when the market looked too risky. The ability to go to "all cash" reduces risks, avoids big losses and actually enables outsized gains during market rebounds.

Most mutual funds are required by their prospectus to stay 70%-98% "fully invested" no matter what the fund manager thinks about the market – bearish or bullish. Investing only in the nine major S&P 500 Sector ETF's, all sectors are invested equally when the market looks bullish. But as any sector's outlook becomes negative, it is immediately sold.

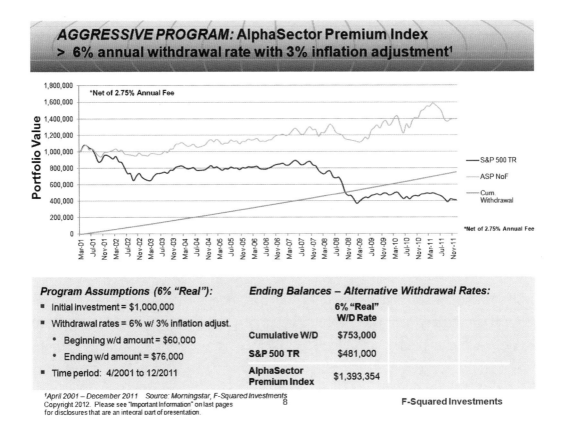

AGGRESSIVE PROGRAM: AlphaSector Premium Index
> 6% annual withdrawal rate with 3% inflation adjustment[1]

Net of 2.75% Annual Fee

Legend: S&P 500 TR — ASP NoF — Cum. Withdrawal

Net of 2.75% Annual Fee

Program Assumptions (6% "Real"):
- Initial investment = $1,000,000
- Withdrawal rates = 6% w/ 3% inflation adjust.
  - Beginning w/d amount = $60,000
  - Ending w/d amount = $76,000
- Time period: 4/2001 to 12/2011

Ending Balances – Alternative Withdrawal Rates:

	6% "Real" W/D Rate
Cumulative W/D	$753,000
S&P 500 TR	$481,000
AlphaSector Premium Index	$1,393,354

[1]April 2001 – December 2011   Source: Morningstar, F-Squared Investments
Copyright 2012. Please see "Important Information" on last pages
for disclosures that are an integral part of presentation.

8

F-Squared Investments

Although nobody can foretell what's going to happen in the market, this manager expects to capture 85% of bull markets while participating in only 15% of market drops. This manager can decide if and when to fully avoid certain market sectors like energy, financials, retail or technology and only invest in other market sectors that look more attractive.

From inception through March 2012, the actual cumulative earnings return was +187% vs. +50.1% in the unmanaged S&P 500 index (which is never able to select specific sectors and avoid less appealing ones, nor can it <u>ever</u> go to "100% cash" in a market-drop or crisis).

Of course, there is NO guarantee that the future will be anything like the past results in any of the four strategies. There WILL BE some fluctuation of account values during a year. However, over the next 5-10 years, using my multi-manager approach, you should expect to safely earn 6½%, 7½% or better annualized returns with <u>two-thirds less</u> stock market risk.

Each of the four money managers can make their own case for successful investing. Another manager chooses just 4-12 select high-yield corporate bond mutual funds out of hundreds of similar funds… and they switch to cash positions when appropriate. **Since their 1998 inception they have <u>never</u> had a negative year (+8.6% -- 13 year average annual return).**

Although only investing in a "single asset class" (or cash), their "favored" funds perform very differently under various economic and interest rate environments - and they take full advantage of that plus enjoy the freedom to go to cash. Their past success of never having a losing year speaks for itself. For the 10 years ending in 12/31/11, the manager's cumulative net returns had gains of +152%… while the far riskier S&P 500 index had only gained +10% over that period.

However, their impressive historical investment performance did not come without minor and brief losses along the way. Since beginning the strategy in 1998, they have had 18 quarters (out of 55 quarters) with a small negative performance. Most of the losing quarters had decreases of less than -1% and the largest quarter's loss ever was a very manageable -2.63%.

With the very real prospects of living a long life, in order to successfully beat inflation, most people will have to take a few carefully chosen and prudent investment risks. I fully believe that my I.R.A. strategy (for taxable brokerage accounts & annuities too) of combining all four investment styles fits the bill - with historically limited and short-term risks to capital.

What's your next step?

You've worked very hard for your money and it took decades to amass your wealth. Unlike many in my generation, you've saved and not squandered. Nor have you piled-up debts to finance a lifestyle that you cannot afford as many younger folks have. No matter how much money you have accumulated, I believe that you still want *all of your assets* to safely work as hard as they can for you, your children and grandchildren.

You'd probably also like your savings to be secure, have instant liquidity should you need it, and want it to safely grow in order to keep pace with rising medical, energy and other living costs.

Let's carefully consider different and prudent investment, financial and tax planning strategies that your current advisor may have never spoken to you about. We won't know for sure which retirement planning ideas might be truly appropriate for you until we discuss your current financial circumstances, your objectives and what is really most important to you. Financial planning is all about the *client's agenda* – not the advisors.

Goals-based financial planning can truly become a collaborative "client-first" endeavor. I will always provide you with comprehensive, easy-to-understand, professional and objective advice. I will only make recommendations that are within your comfort zone: ones that allow you to sleep at night and give you real financial confidence for the future. But be mindful of the real adverse effects of taking no risks at all... due to inflation and your likely longevity. Taking "no risks" could cause you to outlive... your money.

We don't know when the next recession will occur... or the one after that, and the one after that. If you are not totally ready for them, they can ruin both your retirement lifestyle and/or your legacy goals. Why not get prepared with an *all-encompassing conservative retirement plan* in place that is based on your own circumstances, values and goals?

Your monthly income SHOULD increase every year and your wealth should continue to safely grow over time as well *to beat inflation*. We will do our best to safely shield your interest income from falling once again or ever having to deplete your principal to keep up.

If you have $50,000, $100,000 or $1,000,000 of cash sitting in low yielding CD's, bonds or risky mutual funds that you depend on for interest income now... or you just re-invest it, why not explore the multi-faceted "living" benefits of owning a single-pay IUL or whole life policy?

Your life savings can safely grow more quickly than keeping your cash elsewhere while providing for many other financial contingencies too. It's very easy to access this money for any reason. But if you never need to use those assets, they will be multiplied and transferred to your spouse (or loved ones) without any income taxes, probate or delay.

There's no question about the valuable economic value, protection, certainty and peace of mind the tax-free death benefit brings along from day one – especially for a couple who depend on TWO Social Security checks or a pension each month.

Most seniors do not ever calculate the long-term financial impact on the survivor's lifestyle with the permanent loss of one of those monthly checks. Unlike any other assets, the significant life insurance death benefit can offer a remarkable "boost" in this instance and help offset the loss of a monthly Social Security check or monthly pension.

If you do not spend your interest earnings now, **you can *stop writing those annual checks to the I.R.S. to pay unnecessary income taxes and totally avoid those very real lost opportunity costs too***. An IUL or whole life policy will defer those taxes while giving you better opportunities for the safe growth of your cash. Recall that every tax dollar that you pay, but didn't have to, "costs" you the interest you would have earned on it... forever. Over time, this can cost your lifestyle and/or legacy a small fortune.

With an IUL, you can confidently protect these emergency funds on a tax-deferred... or even on a tax-free basis. Doesn't sidestepping all market losses in the bad years, with the potential for locking-in and protecting as much as 12%-14% annual gains in the good years sound more attractive? I call this planning: "control of principal risk and taxation along with real inflation protection". The larger death benefit is what I call the "explosion clause".

Please don't let outdated or pre-conceived notions about life insurance stand in your way of learning more about how these new recession-proof insurance plans can immediately make several simultaneous improvements in your financial well-being. Let's look at your options *given your exact personal situation and objectives* -- and then let's see what you think.

An IUL or special whole life policy *may or may not be part of that plan* or be the best "solution" for you. But have you ever been shown using life insurance as a sound CD and bond alternative before? Do you now realize how many financial areas they can address?

Again, I use many wealth strategies, products and proven money managers to reliably make a positive financial improvement in your life and to better meet your family's goals. However, in most cases, a properly designed single-premium life insurance policy or our select 3rd party money managers will greatly outperform your current investments in the *conservative portion* of your portfolio.

Would you like to find out how much more money we can safely and immediately *increase your monthly interest income by*, given your own specific circumstances? You can confidently enjoy more retirement income today and get better prepared for inflation later.

Maybe you have money invested directly in the stock market now and you are feeling ready to give up the absolutely unpredictable and very risky roller coaster ride, although you are not willing to suffer from low bond interest rates and their price volatility either. I've shown you examples of how well both an IUL and my 3rd party money managers can safely increase your current income and lifestyle… or predictably maximize your wealth and legacy.

The safety of principal, tax-deferral plus the big tax-free death benefit that a "new generation" whole life or an IUL policy offers may be very appealing to you. My low-risk money managers cannot guarantee against some loss of principal, and unless invested inside of an annuity or an I.R.A. they aren't tax-deferred, but their great historical performance should provide reassurance.

How about an annuity you may already own? Can it improved upon to better meet your goals? You may be better off by looking at the new special annuities that triple the value of your account to pay for future LTC expenses (tax-free)… or a special, low-cost annuity that is managed by my "lower-risk" third party money managers.

There are new, fresh options to materially improve on an annuity that you've owned for a while -- whether you want your income right now, can wait for a few more years or hope to never touch those funds at all.

The same would hold true for any existing life insurance policies that you might have. Let's review them too, as you and your heirs might be much better off with a newer one using the latest (least expensive) CSO mortality costs or perhaps get enhanced LTC benefits. You might be very surprised with the results of an audit on any old life insurance policies to increase the death benefit or reduce premiums.

Are you interested in a securing a new guaranteed death benefit policy for handling highly tax-efficient estate and legacy planning goals? I can also help you find the lowest premium available based on your health and lifestyle from very highly-rated insurers. Keep in mind that 2012 is the final year of the I.R.S.'s generous $5,000,000 gift tax exemption. Who knows what the next set of estate tax rules will be in 2013 and beyond?

My clients tell me that my unique financial planning and investment process quickly cuts to the chase of their concerns, needs and goals. Its simplicity makes everything crystal clear. We find out your tolerance for risk and then see how well it matches up with your current portfolio. It usually does not match-up at all. It's hardly ever even close.

Most of the people that I meet with are taking on much more risk than they realize… or feel comfortable with. And they will be very sorry and "stressed-out" during the next bear market and/or recession.

However, a few retirees aren't taking enough prudent risks to meet their current income and lifestyle goals... and are now depleting their principal (with no chance of beating inflation). That's no good either.

We can then carefully compare your current portfolio's past investment performance with the lower-risk portfolio strategies of the 3rd party money managers that we work with. They've all achieved *10+ year NET average returns in the high single-digits with <u>very low volatility and only a few brief, small losses</u>* during the "lost decade" of the 2000's.

If these money managers fit better within your comfort zone and risk parameters, they may become part of our plan to increase your monthly income right away or to safely and steadily grow your wealth. We can get their **investment expertise by moving your I.R.A. to a fee-only I.R.A. account at TCA. For any "non-I.R.A." accounts we can use you choice of either: 1) a *taxable* fee-only TCA advisory account or, 2) a 100% liquid, low-cost, fee-only *tax-deferred* annuity.**

By using the proven concepts in this book, we can predictably grow your nest-egg and bolster your peace of mind. I'm committed to either safely increasing your current income or greatly enlarge your legacy... while adding to your financial flexibility at the same time.

The surest way to be certain that your "safe money" is delivering the fullest value for you, your family or your trust (without taking big market risks) is to closely look at all of your financial options: 1) a *purpose-built* IUL or whole life policy, 2) a more appropriate annuity or perhaps 3) a much more suitable (lower risk) investment portfolio for this point in your life.

There is absolutely no cost or any obligation to explore compelling alternatives to your CD's, bonds, mutual funds and inferior annuities... or just confront your financial worries. Let's examine specific ways to enhance whichever financial area concerns *you* the most.

I do not work for any insurance or investment company. I only work for you. I am completely independent and objective. There is no employer telling me what proprietary financial products or portfolios to "sell" to clients, yet I have a dozen back-office teams to fully support my efforts to serve you and your family well for many years. Working together, we become a "goal focused" team to safely achieve your true financial aspirations.

As an experienced Certified Financial Planner™ I'm a sworn *fiduciary.* This means that I can only recommend sound, dependable financial solutions that are in <u>your</u> best interest -- based solely on your own specific financial values, goals, tolerance for risk and personal circumstances.

Being a *fiduciary*, I am legally held to a much higher and stricter standard of client care than most financial advisors. It's a responsibility and duty that I take seriously. It's the way I've done business since 1997 and all of my clients really appreciate that. So let's get started by discussing what's important to you about your wealth -- and how your income, your overall mix of financial assets and tax situation can work in better harmony with your personal financial priorities and goals. I use a **simple, straightforward yet invaluable *financial planning process* to assist my clients in reaching their goals.**

This proven planning process really works, giving you complete financial confidence and peace of mind. To schedule your free exploratory consultation, simply call my office (770) 777-8309.

In thinking about your own retirement, does it seem "more probable" to you that your money will outlive you… or that you will outlive your money? In either case, we can safely make your life's savings work much harder for you.

Contact me for your FREE "Recession-Proof Retirement" Check-up and a Completely Objective "Safe Money" Review!

Experience a truly unique financial planning process.

Written by Mark J. Orr, CFP®
Certified Financial Planner™
and a fee-based Registered Investment Advisor (RIA)

2050 Marconi Dr. Suite #300   Alpharetta, GA 30005

office (770) 777-8309   mark@SmartFinancesBLOG.com

This book is for general information purposes only, but it is very relevant and extremely useful for most people. However you should consider seeking tax, financial or legal advice from a qualified professional, since the author has no idea of what any individual reader's financial situation, personal circumstances and goals actually are, until we speak.

P.S. – Please help me! If you found the information in this book interesting, thought-provoking, helpful, please share your thoughts and comments on Amazon. Or perhaps you have some constructive criticism so that I may improve the book. Either way, will you please do two things for me?   1) Please write a quick book review on Amazon.com and share your thoughts with potential readers and 2) tell your friends and family about my book too. Thank you very much!

Appendix: Your adult children should really know about IUL's too!

This type of insurance product is not built just for seniors. **Your adult children should learn about using an IUL for their own retirement planning.** With all things considered, it handily beats brokerage accounts, 401(k)s and IRAs by a substantial margin! You'll find some of my client examples below!

In fact, I've written a best-selling book on Kindle just for them. Here's a screenshot of my book on Amazon.com as of 11/01/2012 where it is the Number 1 Kindle eBook in its category of "retirement planning". I will give you the purchase details in a moment. But the following text in this Appendix is taken directly from some pages of that book.

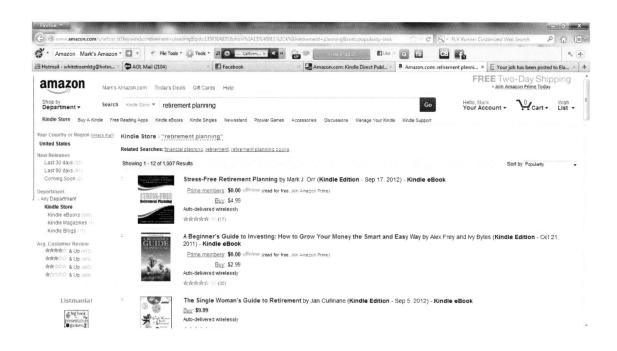

Although the product-type is still an IUL, when I design a policy for someone who is still saving for retirement and accumulating dollars, we simply design the IUL policy differently. By putting in contributions over a period of at least 4 years, we can get TAX-FREE income down the road as well as penalty-free and tax-free access to the money along the way.

The following are some client examples which should be interesting to read.

Jennifer is a 36 year old client who lives in Florida who decided to put away and save $1,000 per month into an IUL until age 66 (with no ongoing obligation to do so). The lowest initial death benefit in her case (according to I.R.S. regulations) starts out at $550,000. The death benefit should grow to over $1.6 million dollars by the time she retires at age 66 because of her combined total of $360,000 in contributions ($12,000 x 30 years) and using historical IUL crediting index interest rates.

Like all life insurance, Jennifer's beneficiary would get a huge death benefit if something awful happened to her – but we're building this policy for LIVING benefits… for her tax-free retirement income or unforeseen financial needs along the way. She can **access most of the policy's cash value in her policy at any time (estimated to be over $475,000 at age 56) and for any purpose** – without taxes or penalties even before retirement.

She can't get that kind of no-penalty or tax-free access from a 401k or IRA. And all along the way, she never has to worry about taking big market risks – or getting access to her money if she ever needs it.

At her retirement age of 67, she could start taking tax-free distributions from her policy of $98,000 per year (growing at 3% a year for the rest of her life – even if she lives to age 103). They would be "income tax-free distributions" because she funded her policy over a period of at least 4-5 years.

But let's say she gets hit by lighting at age 81 – well before her time. **Over just those 15 years she would have received over $1.8 million dollars in tax-free income from her IUL and she would still leave an additional tax-free net death benefit of $1.1 million dollars to her loved ones**. If she didn't pass away at that age, her income could have grown to $152,000 a year (and could still growing by 3% annually for the rest of her life) and she would still leave a substantial death benefit behind.

That's the magic of non-taxed interest compounding over decades. And she's had no market risk along the journey. And did I mention that the cash accumulation and/or death benefit are partially or fully protected from creditors in most states (100% in AL, FL, IL, MO, NC, NJ, NY, TN, TX, etc.)?

I have another 49 year old male client who is making just 4 years of $50,000 annual contributions into his newest IUL (this is his 4th IUL policy with me) for a total of $200,000. He is truly putting his retirement planning on cruise-control – and without any stress due to future bear markets. If we get historical crediting rates that have occurred during the last 25 years on what the raw S&P 500 index did with a 2% floor/12% cap… and he leaves the money alone until age 70, this is what he can expect.

At that point he could start **pulling out over $50,000 tax-free a year (from this policy alone)**. To try to keep up with inflation, that **income amount would grow by 3% every year until age 100**. He could keep taking money out of his policy – without paying taxes for the rest of his life.

If he passes away at age 94, he would have **taken about $1.8 million dollars out of his policy without paying a dime of income taxes and could still leave his spouse a net death benefit of over $460,000**. The longer he lives the better it gets. But should he die very early, his wife will get the $845,000 death benefit.

Now if he had put that $200,000 into a qualified retirement plan like a 401(k) instead, he would have "saved" (really only postponed) $80,000 in taxes (at 40%) over those four years -- but he would pay about $1.3 million in taxes (at 40%) later to net the same $1.8 million in spendable income. Would you rather your children pay only $80,000 in taxes today… or pay $1,300,000 during retirement?

Assuming there aren't any more stock market crashes and no whole decades of "no growth" in the S&P 500 (like 2000-2009), he'd have to pull out about $3.1 million dollars from a 401(k) or an IRA (assuming it was even there!) then pay 40% in taxes, to enjoy the same spendable $1.8 million of total retirement income. I'd like to see ANY 401(k) do that with some market crashes and high fees!

My Kindle book "Stress-Free Retirement Plan" is available at Amazon.com I've written it especially for adults aged from 22-62. You can get it by searching for the blue title above…or have your adult children do a search on Amazon.com for the title so they can download it to their own Kindle, PC, Mac or any tablet (by downloading the FREE Kindle Reader application at Amazon).

Or they can get the brand new paperback version which is also available at Amazon.com.

In fact, many **Fortune 500 companies use high cash value life insurance policies to substantially supplement their top executives' retirement and contribute millions** to fund these plans annually. Small business owners, the wealthy and other savvy people are jumping on the bandwagon too, as they learn about the extraordinary LIVING benefits of a well-designed, maximum-funded IUL contract.

Shouldn't your children explore using the same financial tools as corporate executives the wealthy and successful small business owners?

And your adult children can access their money for any purpose they want, such as emergencies, college education, home improvements or whatever! It's their money and it's easy to get access to most of it, at any time without paying a tax or penalties.

They can't do this with their 401(k) or other qualified plan! There's no application or credit checks to get access to the money in THEIR policy! It just takes a few days to get a check and they never worry about the markets reducing their reserves.

Some of my very smart younger clients even use their IUL as their own "private bank". They borrow money out of their IUL to buy a car and then make their monthly car payments back into their IUL policy -- instead of sending payments to a third party like a bank or credit union.

Why would they do this? **Let me ask you, how much of their monthly car payment do they get to keep (or is returned to them) after they send it to their lender? None... not a penny!** But by taking a loan from their IUL and paying the car payment back into their IUL policy instead of the bank, **not only do they re-capture all of the principal and interest of EACH and every car payment (and their car unlike a lease)... BUT their account is still safely getting market-linked returns of 0-14%.**

So their money is actually working in two places at once. They "pay themselves" the same interest rate as they would to their bank and their policy still earns interest too. I love teaching people these powerful concepts! This really TURBO-charges their personal net worth since they stop transferring their car payments to third parties and keep every dollar of those payments for themselves!

The more people learn about IUL's, the more they come to understand that when fully-funded and structured properly, there is not a more powerful, flexible – yet safe, financial vehicle available.

There are no contribution limits to an IUL whatsoever. But your children, nieces and nephews don't need to be wealthy to benefit from using a properly structured, flexible, investment-grade IUL contract. People with budgets of only $400-500 per month can have a hard time deciding whether to fund a ROTH IRA or an IUL policy, when they weigh ALL of the pros and cons of each.

ROTH IRA's are fine, but they come with too many restrictions. You can only put a maximum of $6,000 a year into one. If you earn too much money then you CAN'T even open one. You need to have "earned" income (you can't fund an IRA for a young child).

And they are still subject to market risk unless they buy fixed annuities or CD's, etc. When one properly designs and fully funds the IUL contract and keeps it in force until death, it can be a very attractive alternative to a ROTH IRA. I call these policies ROTH IRA's on steroids! I'm not wedded to IULs – just great, predictable results!

Most people's money is held in one of three "tax" buckets: taxable, tax-deferred or tax-free. Taxable money is non-qualified brokerage accounts (stocks, bonds and mutual funds), CD's, etc. Tax-deferred accounts are traditional I.R.A.'s, 401(k)'s, annuities, etc. And there are ONLY 3 types of tax-free: ROTH's, muni bonds and cash value permanent life insurance (like an IUL).

Unfortunately, most people have their funds in the wrong places. Too much of their investment cash is in tax-deferred accounts (growing their eventual tax liability) and hardly anything is in a tax-free account. Does that make sense to you?

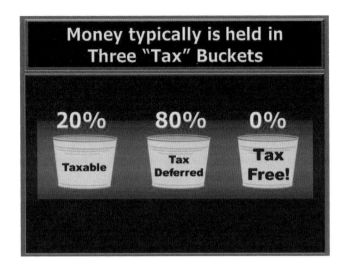 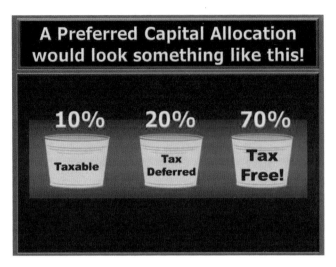

Your adult children can greatly benefit from an IUL where they can avoid all market losses, earn potential double-digit gains when the market does well and lock those gains in and protect them from future bear market losses. ROTH's don't have the "reset mechanism" either - allowing them to profit during market rebounds!

Unlike brokerage accounts, they pay no income taxes during the time they are accumulating their savings. And unlike IRA's or 401(K)s, if they ever need to access their funds they can sidestep taxes and penalties and get to most all of their cash in a matter of days.

And down the road, when they want a monthly "retirement paycheck", **they can get tax-free income like they could with a ROTH IRA, as long as they follow the simple I.R.S. rules**. But if the worst ever happened along the way, their loved ones would be well-protected by the tax-free death benefit.

There are so many advantages over other savings vehicles that everyone should at least explore owning an IUL! Encourage your adult children to get and READ a copy of my book, the **"Stress-Free Retirement Planning"**. They will thank you for introducing this strategy to them.

I can help your kids "find the money" to save and invest?

Throughout their lifetime, only a certain amount of money will flow through their hands (and bank account). Most of this money will certainly come from their job (salary, commissions, bonuses, etc.) or profits from their business. Some will come from earnings on their investments. Some may come from an inheritance. For a few of them it will be a little amount of money, for many of them it will be an average amount and for the rest of them, it will be a great deal of money.

They can try to increase it but it will still be a finite sum that they should be careful with. Once spent, they can't get that dollar back. I always advise that they should make every dollar that they get work as hard as possible for them.

But believe it or not, for most of the Americans that will be reading this book, it will be millions of dollars that are going to come to them over their lifetime. How they spend, save and invest those millions of dollars will ultimately determine not only their financial freedom, comfort and lifestyle today, but their future retirement lifestyle, peace of mind and the ultimate legacy they will leave for their own family and loved ones.

Those dollars will also determine how easily they will get through the economic recessions that occur every 5-6 years and how much they can share with others or charities that they feel strongly about. Help them make the most of those dollars. These safe financial strategies and opportunities can make a substantial difference in their life with very little effort on their part

So another unique feature of my financial planning practice is that **I can actually help them "FIND THE MONEY" to fund their IUL and actually empower their retirement dreams (or even help them pay off their home and all other debts in as little as 5-11 years) – WITHOUT REDUCING their present lifestyle**.

All most other financial advisors want to talk to them about, is their "accumulated money" (CD's, an old 401(k), I.R.A.s, brokerage accounts and annuities) and then <u>moving</u> them under their management. I can do a great job for them with that as well. But I want to give them their financial life back!

That's right, my other expertise lies in eliminating their "transferred money" – this is money that they are unknowingly or unnecessarily transferring away to 3rd parties year after year. Like how they pay for their home, their cars, credit card debts, pay their taxes, fund their children's education and prepare for their own retirement, etc. (all of these are called permanent wealth transfers). That's financial transformation.

I can easily help them to get completely out of debt and then we take that new "found" money and put most of it into their retirement savings and improve their current lifestyle with the rest. I often <u>find a total</u> of $10,000's or even $100,000 or more money that can fund both an IUL and a better current lifestyle.

This part of my financial practice is perhaps the most time-consuming, yet rewarding. I cannot tell you what it feels like to take a person or family from financial discouragement and hopelessness… to being completely optimistic and truly looking forward to their future with no fear. We put a real plan in place to get control of their financial life right now and forever. There are others out there that teach similar or part of these financial concepts like Dave Ramsey and some guy that constantly advertises on the radio.

Dave Ramsey's method for quickly getting out of debt is only half right– he's left out a powerful factor of debt acceleration and then building lasting wealth. His generic advice is worthwhile and for a few bucks on Amazon.com, you get started with his "workbook". But I'm guessing that up to 50%-65% of his readers can get out of debt quicker and start building wealth sooner with our more encompassing strategies.

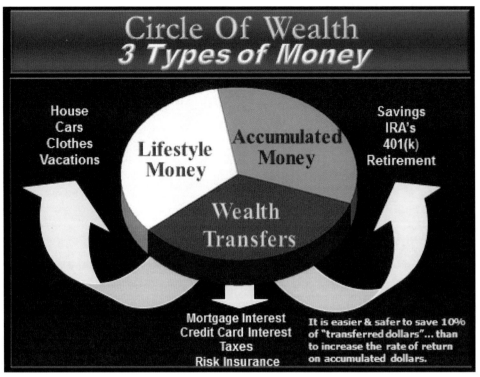

I can help them FIND THE MONEY --
Without Reducing Their Present Lifestyle

Dave Ramsey's method for quickly getting out of debt is only half right– he's left out the most powerful factor of debt acceleration and then building lasting wealth.

His generic advice is worthwhile and for a few bucks on Amazon.com, you get started with his "workbook". But I'm guessing that up to 50%-65% of his readers can get out of debt quicker and start building wealth sooner with our more encompassing methods and strategies.

Save more and enjoy life more – on the same income as they have now. How much money can I "find" for their future retirement? I can help them "power down" their debt load and empower their own financial freedom sooner than you think. We're not magicians, but we do this every week for our clients. Most advisors have no idea how to help you do this, but that's the subject of another upcoming book.

I might remind my readers that having "financial issues" are the number one cause of divorce in this country. Personal financial problems are also one of the biggest causes of lack of productivity in the office as well. Now I'm certainly not suggesting that I can save anyone's marriage, or keep all employees 100% focused on their jobs while at work, but helping my clients eliminate debt and get more security and financial peace of mind can do wonders for most couples.

What if I've been working with your children for 8 years and we have paid off all of their debts, including their mortgage, on the same payments that they are currently making today? And they now don't owe anything to anybody. How good would that make them feel? What kind of financial confidence and freedom would that give them?

Again, I encourage you to have them get and then READ my "<u>Stress-Free Retirement Planning</u>" book (see the front cover right below). They can search for the Kindle version or paperback of that title on Amazon. If they take the information contained in the book to heart, it can and will change their lives forever, and that of your grandchildren.

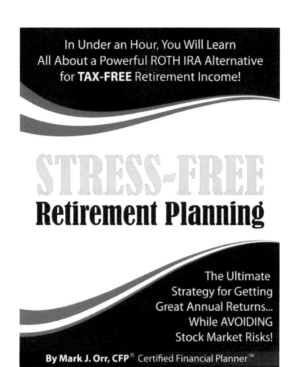

Of course, you or they can contact me directly with any questions:

Mark J. Orr, CFP®

Certified Financial Planner™
and a fee-based **Registered Investment Advisor**

2050 Marconi Drive Suite #300   Alpharetta, GA 30005
770-777-8309

About the Author:

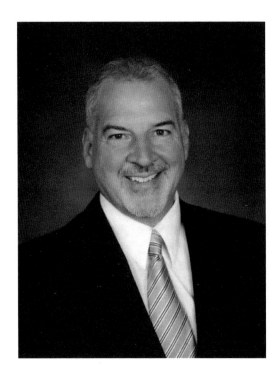

Mark has been a practicing Certified Financial Planner since 2000. Certified Financial Planners are held to the strictest ethical standards and must study for two years prior to taking a 10 hour exam that less than 65% of test takers pass the first time. Since 1997, he has held life, health and variable insurance licenses and the Series 7 Securities license and became a Registered Investment Advisor representative.

He began his financial services career as a Long Term Care Insurance Specialist in 1997and has greatly expanded his practice to better serve his clients since then. In 2007, he opened up his own fee-based Registered Investment Advisory business, MORR Capital Management, Inc.

Through this firm, he manages client assets – primarily using proven third party money managers. These accounts are allocated in portfolios based on a clients' tolerance for risk, time horizon and investment goals. In July 2012, he gave up his Series 7 securities (stockbrokers) license since he felt that it was in direct conflict with his registered investment advisory business and his core beliefs as a fiduciary.

He is the author of several e-books and Special Reports. He has led dozens and dozens of public seminars on various financial topics as well as being interviewed as a guest on several morning radio shows.

Prior to entering the financial services business, Mark spent the early part of his career in the luxury resort real estate marketing and development industry – both in America and in Europe.

He is a two-time past board member of his local Rotary Club and continues to be active in community service through the Rotary Club and other community affairs. On a personal note, Mark and Norma love to travel – especially to warm sandy beaches in the sun and cruises. Staying in good shape is important to him and he enjoys good red wine. Finally, he is the proud father of three grown children (Megan, Marina and Michael) and a wonderful grandson (Grayson).

Made in the USA
San Bernardino, CA
18 December 2012